The Internal Economy

*how to apply market principles within organizations
to make sense of budgeting, rate-setting,
project-approval, and accounting processes*

by

N. Dean Meyer

The Internal Economy: how to apply market principles within organizations to make sense of budgeting, rate-setting, project-approval, and accounting processes

Meyer, N. Dean

Key words: budget, rates, prices, chargebacks, cost allocations, priority setting, project-approval process, accounting, financial metrics, shared services, entrepreneurship, governance, strategic alignment.

NDMA Publishing
641 Danbury Road, Suite D
Ridgefield, CT 06877 USA

203-431-0029
ndma@ndma.com

ISBN   1-892606-18-6

Printed in the United States of America.

BOOKS BY N. DEAN MEYER

COMPANION TO THIS BOOK:
The Internal Economy: Overview of Implementation Processes.
2002

Monograph describing the stages of evolution of an internal economy, from "Centrally Planned" to "Fee For Service" (charge-backs). Also describes step-by-step implementation processes both for Budget-by-Deliverables and for the broader internal economy systems and processes.

ALSO AUGMENTING THIS BOOK:
An Introduction to Activity-based Budgeting. 2002

Monograph explaining the ABC's of activity-based costing, and how it's applied to budgeting and pricing. Leads to fiscally sound budget decisions, a match between clients' expectations and available resources, and rates based on full cost.

Downsizing Without Destroying: how to trim what your organization does rather than destroy its ability to do anything at all. 2003

Monograph exploring approaches to downsizing in tough times, why conventional approaches are destructive, and a sensible alternative based on business strategy and portfolio management that can trim what an organization does rather than destroy its ability to do anything at all.

An Introduction to the Business-Within-a-Business Paradigm.
2002

Monograph describing a compelling vision of high-performance organizations and its implications for governance.

RoadMap: how to understand, diagnose, and fix your organization. 1998.

The fundamental systems within organizations, and how to plan a transformation process that converts traditional organizations into entrepreneurial businesses within a business.

Fast Track to Changing Corporate Culture. 2003

Monograph on how to drive dramatic changes in corporate culture in less than a year, addressing teamwork, customer focus, entrepreneurship, empowerment, integrity, and interpersonal relations.

Meyer's Rules of Order: how to hold highly productive business meetings. 2001

A little pocket book of simple, pragmatic guidelines that can dramatically improve the effectiveness of all business meetings; includes effective method for consensus decision making.

The Building Blocks Approach to Organization Charts. 2002.

The science of designing entrepreneurial organization charts, including the basic building blocks of structure and principles for combining them into healthy organizations; also describes processes for dynamic, cross-boundary work-flows.

Outsourcing: how to make vendors work for your shareholders. 1999.

A critical analysis of the claims of outsourcing vendors, a review of the real reasons for outsourcing, and an approach to managing vendors through (not around) internal staff.

Decentralization: Fantasies, Failings, and Fundamentals. 1998.

Why decentralization is so expensive and harmful, why people advocate it, and how to get the benefits without paying the costs.

The New Lexicon of Leadership: dictionary of terms used in leadership and organizational design. 2003.

A glossary of business terms that are critical to clear communications and clear thinking about organizations and leadership, especially useful in participative processes of change.

The Information Edge with Mary E. Boone. 1987.

How to find and measure the strategic benefits of information systems (with over sixty case studies).

To Jodi,
and to enjoying
the adventure
in each day.

CONTENTS

FIGURES

The Internal Economy

*how to apply market principles within organizations
to make sense of budgeting, rate-setting,
project-approval, and accounting processes*

FOREWORD: Why Should I Care?

Your organization's resource-management processes are extremely important for two reasons:

1. They determine whether or not your organization is well aligned with corporate strategies.

2. They have a major impact on the organization's effectiveness, reputation, and the quality of work life of its staff.

Since this book is about organizational processes, I must be careful to define the term. By "organization" I mean any group of people working together to achieve a common and ongoing purpose.

In this book, the term "corporation" will refer to an entire institution. In this usage, a corporation may be a conglomerate or a company, a government agency, a university, a union, a charity, or a faith-based fellowship. It may seek to make a profit, or it may be not-for-profit.

Within corporations are "organizations." An example of an organization within a corporation is a service department such as engineering, manufacturing, finance, or IT.

Organizations exist to serve "clients" — people who benefit from their work. *1*

An organization whose primary business is serving people within the same corporation is termed an "internal service provider."

While the concepts in this book apply to entire corporations, they're generally implemented one organization at a time. Therefore, this book will focus on internal service providers within corporations.

---

1.   "Clients" are customers outside the organization. Other managers within the organization may also be customers (though they are not clients). The word "staff" will be used to refer to people within the organization.

Back to the two reasons why you should care about your organization's resource-management processes: strategic alignment; and effectiveness, reputation, and staff's quality of work life.

With regard to strategic alignment, an organization maximizes its value to its clients when its priorities match theirs. Aligned priorities result from the processes that determine what an organization's finite resources (money and people's time) are spent on.

With regard to effectiveness, reputation, and quality of work life, clients' expectations have to fit within an organization's resources. Otherwise, staff will burn out trying to fulfill demands well beyond their resources. In spite of their heroic efforts, they'll fail to fulfill their committments and they'll be blamed for unresponsiveness or unreliability.

Furthermore, careers will be crippled when people are so busy scrambling to keep up with clients' excessive demands that they don't have time for professional development and product R&D. In the short term, staff become less effective. Ultimately, their skills become obsolete and people burn out.

Note that effectiveness, reputation, and quality of work life also come down to alignment, in this case, of clients' expectations (demand) with the organization's resources (supply).

So much depends on how well an organization's resources are aligned with well-chosen client priorities and expectations.

And there's more....

In addition to serving individual clients, most organizations perform some "corporate-good" activities and also pursue projects that are investments in the organization itself. Somehow an organization must designate the right amount of funding for each of these purposes.

Meanwhile, managers within the organization need information on their resources to make decisions and to evaluate their subordinates. Executives must ensure that an organization stays within its budget.

Clients need to know what they're getting for their money. And all this information must be integrated with corporate accounting systems.

All these fundamental governance challenges are part of the design of an organization's resource-management processes.

Strategic contribution, reputation, quality of work life... so much depends on how well an organization's resources are aligned with well-chosen client priorities and expectations.

The impacts of poorly designed resource-management processes are felt throughout a corporation. Poor decisions lead to low payoff. And an imbalance between demand and supply (between expectations and resources) creates a contentious and demotivational environment for both clients and staff.

On the other hand, when they're well designed, all these processes work in concert to channel scarce resources to the places that need them the most. The right people are empowered to control resources, and they have the information they need to make fiscally sound decisions in keeping with business strategies. And everyone understands just what will and won't be done with the organization's finite resources.

Instead of battling resource-management issues one budget, one project approval or investment decision, one client dispute at a time, this book explains how to design the whole set of resource-management processes — from budgeting through spending decisions to accounting — as an effective, integrated system.

1. Introduction:
What's In This Book

The sad truth is, many organizations entangle themselves in ineffective, bureaucratic resource-management processes. And it seems that whenever anyone tries to improve them, they only get more convoluted.

Too often, budget decisions are arbitrarily based on prior year's budgets, without regard for investment opportunities in the coming year or the needs of business strategies. Priorities are disjointed and conflicting. Managers are rewarded for building empires. Oversight committees disempower those who are best positioned to manage their professions. Policies are issued, then ignored.

The result is wasted time, poor decision making that reduces shareholder value, 2 missed strategic opportunities as resources go to the wrong things, and strained relations between internal service providers and their clients.

There's no shortage of evidence of this unfortunate reality. Talk to the head of any corporate service function — be it IT, Finance, HR, Marketing, Engineering, whatever — and you'll hear concern for the way resources are governed.

The good news is, there *is* a rational, methodical way to design effective resource-management processes. The resulting processes are generally simpler, make sense to people, solve real problems, and improve fiscal decision making and bottom-line results.

This book starts with the reality of today's typical resource-management practices and explores the problems they create.

---

2.   In not-for-profit organizations, interpret "shareholder value" and "profits" to mean the extent to which the institution achieves its mission at a given level of funding.

Then, it puts a fresh perspective on the entire set of resource-management processes — putting them all in the context of a "business within a business" facing a marketplace of customers. It applies *market economics to the design of resource-management processes within organizations.*

Making theory practical, it explains the various components of a market economy as applied within organizations and how they should work when put into practice in the real world.

Finally, the book summarizes the benefits of a market-based approach, and its implications for corporate governance and for leadership.

For those who are interested, a companion monograph explains how to implement a market-based internal economy. [3]

There is a rational, methodical way to design effective resource-management processes.

The Internal Economy applies well-established economic theory in a new way. In doing so, it brings clear vision to complex and controversial governance issues such as the design of budgeting processes; priority-setting and project-approval processes; allocations, chargebacks, and the determination of rates; and financial metrics.

Although the theory described in this book is innovative and far reaching, the recommendations are practical and accessible. The result is a pragmatic solution that can lead to breakthroughs on very real leadership issues.

3.   Meyer, N. Dean. *The Internal Economy: overview of implementation processes.* Ridgefield, CT: NDMA Publishing. 2004.

2. Reality: Convoluted Resource-management Processes

Very few organizations have consciously planned their resource-management processes based on principles and methodical design.

This chapter describes what typically goes wrong, and the consequences of those design flaws.

Of course, there are myriad things that can go wrong. Only the most common and the most painful dysfunctions are illustrated here.

Why dwell on the problems of the past? Understanding the root cause of common problems will help leaders design lasting systemic solutions.

It Starts With the Budget

Pat manages a corporate service function. In her company, tremendous effort is expended preparing and defending budgets for the coming year. Nonetheless, Pat's staff are cynical because all their hard work seems to have little impact on budget decisions.

Here's how it works:

Pat sets up a budget spreadsheet.

*   The *columns represent cost factors* (expense codes) such as salaries, travel expenses, professional development, vendor services, etc.

*   The *rows represent deliverables* — specific projects and services that her organization plans to produce in the coming fiscal year.

Her budget spreadsheet looks something like this:

	Salaries	Travel	Training...
Project 1	$	$	$
Project 2	$	$	$
Service 3	$	$	$
Service 4	$	$	$

After filling in this spreadsheet, she *totals the columns*. The line items in the budget she submits are for compensation, travel, training, etc.

In other words, in Pat's company, budgets describe *cost factors* for each group in her organization. They do not describe the total cost of each *deliverable* across all groups that participate in each project team (the row totals).

Presenting a budget in this traditional way invites the wrong kind of dialog. Executives debate Pat's travel and training expenses, micro-managing her in a way they would never do to an external vendor.

Executives debate travel and training expenses, micro-managing staff.

Obviously, these corporate executives are not well qualified to decide how much travel and training Pat actually needs to stay in business; but they've got to trim something and Pat's given them nothing else to look at.

Typically, the first thing to go is necessary investments in her staff. To do her job, Pat knows her people need a modicum of training and consulting assistance. But in the budget process, most of her funding for training, travel, and consulting are cut.

As you might expect, no one grants that this may impact her department's productivity and future viability, so expectations remain high.

Busy micro-managing her, corporate executives are *not* making the kind of decisions they ought to. They should be examining investment opportunities and channeling scarce corporate resources into the most strategic projects. And they should be funding strategic initiatives across all the various corporate departments that need to be involved to deliver each corporate strategy, not looking at Pat's budget in isolation.

But executives can't make strategic investments when looking at a budget of cost factors by group. So they decide each group's budget by comparing its cost factors to prior years.

This completely frustrates Pat. She knows her organization could deliver many high-payoff projects in the coming year. But she's left alone trying to defend budget increases. Her clients — the business units — feel that it's her job to get enough money to satisfy all their needs. After all, they can't defend her travel and training budgets.

Obviously, Pat has a vested interest in maximizing her budget (or so people think). So her arguments are unconvincing, and corporate executives continue to cut her budget request, even though doing so forgoes some really great opportunities.

In spite of her pleas, Pat's budget is decided based on last year's level plus or minus a few percent (perhaps adjusted to accommodate a few large projects), or on available supply (what can her current headcount handle), or on other extraneous factors such as political clout or salesmanship.

This arbitrary number has little relationship to business strategies or to the investment opportunities at hand.

What if most of the proposed projects *aren't* worth doing? If it adds up to roughly the same as last year, it must be okay!

Or what if *all* are great investments? New investments, however lucrative, are discouraged because they're "over budget."

Budget decisions have little relationship to business strategies or to the investment opportunities at hand.

Privately, everyone would admit that this traditional budget process is bad for the bottom line. Shareholders may be missing great investment opportunities in one area, while funding low-payoff work in another.

But it's the best that corporate executives can do with the information they're given.

Impossible Expectations

The new fiscal year begins where the last ended: at warp speed. Clients' demands far outstrip Pat's available resources.

At this point, Pat knows the size of her budget. (And she knows her staff can't travel anywhere for at least a year.) But nobody has a clue about which projects and services are covered by her budget.

Not knowing any better, clients feel that it's up to her to get whatever resources are required to satisfy them. They say, "We gave you all that money in your budget. Now we expect you to fulfill all our needs."

In other words, the corporation gives Pat a finite amount of money in her budget; and, in trade, clients expect infinite services — anything people might ask for throughout the year!

In the face of this unrealistic backlog, Pat has no basis for saying, "That wasn't covered in our budget. We'll need incremental resources to do it."

Nobody knows what's covered in the budget and what's not.

Of course, clients blame Pat when her organization can't produce everything they demand.

Success in this situation is impossible. Ultimately, Pat becomes a scapegoat. The year has barely begun, and pondering how she'll satisfy client demands with her limited budget, Pat knows she's heading for trouble.

Insufficient Reinvestment in the Organization

With clients screaming, "But I need it!" Pat's staff feel pressured to make promises beyond their capacity to deliver.

Then, they scramble to meet those impossible commitments. But in spite of putting in long hours, they still cannot possibly satisfy clients' demands.

This gap between clients' demands and available resources is demoralizing. As hard as they may work, staff get blamed for unresponsiveness and unreliability. It's a no-win situation that's stressful and unproductive.

Under unreasonable pressure to deliver results, Pat's staff spend every minute working on current projects. (Some even burn themselves out working nights and weekends.)

Under unreasonable pressure to deliver results to clients, staff take little time for professional development, product research, or spending time with clients.

They have no time to keep their skills, knowledge, and product lines up to date; they don't have time to work on new project proposals; they don't even have time to answer clients' voice mail. By not looking after their own futures, they're "eating their seed corn."

In the long run, Pat's organization is not able to maintain its capabilities. Her staff's skills fall behind, her technologies become obsolete, and her infrastructure becomes overstressed and fragile.

For good reason, Pat's department is accused of being out of date and difficult to do business with.

New Business

Pat does have one client with whom she gets along well. Fortunately, it's one of the growth business units with plenty of cash, and its leaders agree to fund a few key projects with their considerable budget.

Pat hopes this influx of additional money will give her a little relief.

In fact, it does just the opposite. Consider what she charges for this incremental work:

Her prices *should* be calculated to include all the right costs — both direct costs and a fair share of indirect costs and overhead. Direct costs are easy. But if any indirect costs are left out (and they always are, Pat reflects), her prices are unrealistically low.

As clients buy more, direct costs (like contractors) are covered, but indirect costs (like internal support functions) are not. Support groups within her organization lack resources to grow and become strained.

Indirect (so-called "fixed") resources like management and infrastructure feel the strain most.

Beyond that, everybody feels it in their own way. Some portion of staff's time has to be set aside for administration, professional development, client support — a variety of "unbillable" activities. The amount of unbillable time Pat had funded in her budget was already way too low. And now, as her business grows, this fixed amount is spread even more thinly.

Surprisingly, the additional revenues Pat gets from her friendly clients turn out to hurt more than help her.

Giving Away the Infrastructure

Meanwhile, Pat's infrastructure desperately needs upgrading. But in her company, budget for infrastructure is justified as part of clients' projects.

Of course, each project proposal includes only the minimum in capital to satisfy its immediate needs. So Pat is forced to buy capacity in small chunks.

Later, having "paid for" pieces of her infrastructure via their projects, clients justifiably feel they have the right to control it.

Many of her machines are running well below full capacity. But when she tries to optimize enterprisewide capacity and share infrastructure among clients to gain economies of scale, clients demand that she leave "their" machines alone.

Her capabilities, both people and infrastructure, continue to deteriorate over time.

The insidious impacts of this traditional budget process don't stop here.

Differing Priorities Undermine Teamwork

Pat does her best to ensure that priorities are clear to her staff, at least among clients projects. But her managers still seem to be working at cross purposes. In particular, her priorities aren't relevant to support groups within her organization who don't work directly on these client projects.

The problem is, each of her managers has his or her own budget and each independently sets priorities for his or her group. One's highest priority may be a support group's lowest, so teamwork breaks down and critical projects are delayed.

Pat spends what little training money she can scrape together on a team-building retreat which everybody enjoys. But the ultimate effect on teamwork is minimal. Priorities still differ and groups still can't get the support they need from their peers.

Changing Priorities

Of course, the world is always changing, and priorities must be adjusted throughout the year.

As new strategic imperatives arise, somebody has to revise priorities. With no defined process, Pat steps in to fill the vacuum.

Pat adjusts her organization's priorities with trepidation, fearing that when money is channeled away from the projects discussed during the budget process to higher priority things which arose mid-year, no matter how good the reason, she'll be faulted for not doing everything she promised last year when she defended her budget.

There's another reason she feels troubled. In setting priorities, she has to assess the wisdom and value of clients' requests, and finds herself *judging* their ideas. Clearly, this is the opposite of customer focus. Clients see Pat as an obstacle that has to be overcome, not on their side of the table.

At a minimum, this arm's-length relationship constrains her ability to participate in clients' strategic thinking. They "get their act together" before bringing her in.

Worse, clients resent being disempowered. They view it as a vendor deciding what they'll buy. As a result, clients advocate decentralization or outsourcing, both of which put them back in the role of valued customers who are in control of their priorities and purchase decisions.

Confusing Project-approval Processes

Since Pat's project approval (priority setting) processes evolved in an ad hoc manner, they are vague and overly complex. Big investments go one route, while small projects go another. Some decisions are made at Pat's level, and others are made by her managers. Decisions lack objective criteria and are inconsistent.

Some clients don't feel heard, and believe that the only way to get things done is to play politics or beg favors from the right person.

When decisions rise to her level, Pat admits she's not really in the best position to know the needs of her clients. While she has a great understanding of the corporation's overall business, she can never know clients businesses, strategies, and needs as well as they do. Yet she still has to set priorities.

She gets some guidance from the company's strategic plan, from the discussions she had with her peers during the budget process, and from her participation on the corporate executive team throughout the year. But even with all this input, she's not comfortable that she's making the best decisions for the corporation.

As a result, Pat really can't be certain that her organization's activities are well aligned with the corporation's business strategies. In her heart, she knows that the corporation may be spending some of its resources on the wrong things.

Steering Committee

At this point, Pat's boss "strongly urges" her to form a client steering committee as part of her "governance" processes.

Pat breathes a sigh of relief. At least this gets her out of the hot-seat of telling clients "no."

A committee of corporate executives is established to decide her organization's priorities. Pat tries to support them, and sets up a project-approval process that requires the committee's approval for all significant investments. (She defines "significant" as anything over a certain cost threshhold.)

Pat knows that the committee members are closer to the business than she is, but she soon sees that they're not necessarily making better decisions than she did. Their discussions seem shallow. Committee members rarely take the time to understand the strategic implications of each and every project. At times, decision-making seems more political than analytical, as if executives are privately saying, "I'll approve yours if you support mine."

But at least she's no longer to blame when clients don't get what they want (she hopes).

The committee does set priorities, putting projects in sequence. But Pat is disappointed to observe that the committee doesn't help her manage clients' expectations to fit within her available resources.

For one thing, the committee has no sense of the full cost of each project (including support groups), and it doesn't have a clear understanding of its spending power — the resources in Pat's organization which are available to do the projects (those not absorbed by ongoing operations).

Thus, even though priorities are clear, no one knows just how many of the projects on the list can actually be accomplished — that is, where the line will be drawn. As a result, clients still expect more than Pat has resources to deliver.

There's another problem with setting priorities without an understanding of where the line will be drawn. What if they had $10 million to spend (Pat's total budget), and their choices (in priority sequence) were as follows:

      Project 1:   cost $9 million, payoff $12 million
      Project 2:   cost $5 million, payoff $8 million
      Project 3:   cost $4 million, payoff $6 million

Note that, within the available budget, the organization can either do Project 1 alone (payoff $12), or both Project 2 and Project 3 (total payoff $14). Just working down the priority list can lead to the wrong answer. If costs and spending power were known, the committee's decisions might be different.

To make matters worse, most clients avoid having to go through the committee whenever possible by breaking up their projects into a series of small steps, each of which is under the threshhold. Although the committee thinks it has all her resources to prioritize, most of her staff's hours seem to leak away fulfilling all these little requests.

Soon it becomes evident that Pat's staff is not delivering the projects the committee thought it had approved, and questions about her organization's performance are raised.

To her dismay, it's not long before the committee goes beyond its role of priority setting and demands to review Pat's strategies, technical decisions, and internal management initiatives.

With them micro-managing her every move in a spirit of mistrust, Pat finds herself disempowered and has difficulty implementing the kinds of changes she knows her department needs.

Failure at Strategic Leadership

In addition to supplying products and services to clients, Pat's organization does some things for the good of the corporation as a whole. Staff are involved in policy planning, vendor product reviews, and corporate initiatives like the United Way.

The costs of these "corporate-good" activities are invisible in her budget. Therefore, when clients consider what they're getting for the money, internal staff appear to be more expensive than outsourcing because these other costs (which vendors don't have to incur) are buried in her prices. This puts her entire organization in a bad light.

Pat has no choice but to keep these corporate-good functions to a minimum. Lacking time to get involved, she drops out of many corporate policy committees, and spends little time on community-action programs that most senior executives volunteer to do. As a result, Pat drifts away from her peers on the executive team.

Corporate executives conveniently forget that they cut her budget to bare bones, and quietly criticize Pat for not providing the kind of corporatewide leadership they expect from her.

Disempowered Bureaucrats

Pat becomes very discouraged as she thinks about her deteriorating client relationships and reputation. So she turns her reflection inward to her own staff who at least are loyal to her.

Instead of lifting her spirits, her shift in focus only reveals more worries.

While they'd never openly admit it, Pat's managers feel that the way to get ahead is to maximize their budgets and then make sure the money is used up by year end (i.e., spend, not save, money). It's not that they're bad managers. The unfortunate truth is, the bigger their budget, the higher their job grade.

Financial reports don't tell Pat whether her managers are running cost-effective businesses, or delivering anything at all, for that matter. These reports only tell her whether managers are spending as much as they said they would.

Since the metrics don't ensure performance but do encourage empire building, Pat feels the need to micro-manage her staff. Her only hope for ensuring productivity is to get involved in detailed reviews of projects, milestones, and staffing decisions. The whole system induces disempowerment.

The system also undermines entrepreneurship. Pat knows to the penny how well her managers' actual expenses match their budgets, but she can't compare their costs to the value they deliver. Put simply, she tracks their expenses but not their results.

A manager who spends exactly what was budgeted but produces very little appears, on the surface, to be performing well ("coming in on budget"). On the other hand, a manager who attracts a lot of business, and spends more to deliver more, earns the stigma of a negative budget variance to be explained.

As a result, her managers are reluctant to expand staff (e.g., through contractors) to meet new clients' demands, even if clients are willing to provide the money. They turn away paying customers in order to adhere to their original budgets.

In this cost-conscious environment, Pat doesn't feel she can preach a culture of creative, proactive entrepreneurship which might bring in more business, even if it were to result in big payoffs for shareholders. It would not seem politically correct.

Cutting Costs Inevitably Cuts Capabilities

Mid year, profits come under pressure and a corporate mandate prohibits everybody from spending money on travel or consultants. What little that had been approved in her budget is now frozen.

Nonetheless, clients still expect Pat to deliver a highly visible project which requires her staff to visit corporate sites globally, and which depends on external consultants for new technologies.

With little thought among her peers as to why, Pat is blamed when this project fails.

As the corporation's profit picture continues to deteriorate, Pat's budget is reduced still further. Of course, everyone expects her to continue delivering all the same products and services, as if she had a lot of "fat" in her budget that could be trimmed without threatening results.

Pat turns to her steering committee for help. Instead of taking things off her plate, they start to discuss which positions in her organization should be eliminated in order to save money. This isn't the kind of help she had in mind!

The cuts inevitably reduce her capabilities, but in a haphazard rather than well-planned way. Taking a little bit out of every group makes the entire organization less productive, and every project is adversely affected.

Since expectations weren't cut to match reduced resources, Pat is blamed when virtually all her organization's projects come in late or aren't delivered at all. *4*

Allocations

At the end of the year, the corporation distributes Pat's costs through allocations to the business units — high-level formulas that people find difficult to understand.

Just as she's heading into the new fiscal year, allocations remind everybody of how expensive her department is. Her peers at the executive level see costs, not benefits, because the results of most of her organization's work are delivered at lower levels within their business units.

Costs, not benefits.... Of course Pat's department seems too expensive!

Pat scrambles to explain all the deliverables they got for their money. It's not easy, since deliverables are not clearly documented or linked to her budget. In response, her peers seem skeptical.

Perhaps worse, business unit leaders resent getting hit with costs they can't control. They see it as "taxation without representation" and fight back. They claim that Pat overcharged them to subsidize others, or that they're being unfairly charged for things they didn't agree to buy.

The allocations invariably fire up fruitless political controversies that keep Pat scrambling for weeks. The end result is a lot of wasted time and angst. The entire process leaves executives filled with doubts and suspicions, not the kind of relationships Pat's career needs.

4.   For more on downsizing approaches, good and bad, see: Meyer, N. Dean. *Downsizing Without Destroying: how to trim what your organization does rather than destroy its ability to do anything at all.* Ridgefield, CT: NDMA Publishing. 2003.

What's Going On Here?

Is Pat a "performance problem" and a liability to her boss?

It sure looks that way.

Pat tried hard, and utilized what many would consider "best practices." Her financial and technical decisions were reasonably good, and her staff produced a lot of good work on a limited budget.

The problem is, she's a victim of her organization's resource-management processes — and she hasn't taken the initiative to fix them.

Certainly no one is stopping Pat from taking the initiative. Why wouldn't she?

Perhaps she didn't recognize the importance of doing so. The next chapter briefly summarizes the reasons for change, i.e., the symptoms that indicate dysfunctional resource-management processes.

Or perhaps Pat just didn't know what to do. The rest of this book explains how to design highly effective resource-management processes.

3. Problem Statement:
Symptoms That Can Be Fixed

Is fixing your resource-management processes worth the effort?

If Pat's plight didn't convince you, consider just a few of the problems that are created by ineffective resource-management processes, all of which *can* be fixed in a rational, systematic way:

* Budgets are based on arbitrary benchmarks such as last year's level. As a result, budget levels may be too low (forgoing good investments) or too high (permitting low-payoff work).

* In the budget process, executives may micro-manage organizations, dictating specific cost factors like travel and training budgets. Not well equiped to do so, they make poor decisions and undermine staff's effectiveness.

* Insufficient reinvestment in staff's capabilities (e.g., training, product development) leads to obsolescence and turnover.

* Without knowing what is and what's not covered by the budget, clients demand more than staff can deliver, and then blame staff when they don't get all they want.

* When priority decisions are made only once a year during the budget process, an organization cannot respond to rapid shifts in business strategies. As a result, its strategic alignment and contribution to shareholder value — indeed, its relevance — deteriorate steadily through the year.

* When managers within an organization judge clients' requests and set their own priorities, customer-focus fades and clients' resentment grows. As a result, partnerships are undermined and strategic alignment becomes even more difficult.

* Differing priorities among the managers within an organization undermine teamwork, since one group's highest priority may be a support-group's lowest.

* Staff are expected to match costs to budgets (actuals to plans) rather than to run cost-effective businesses. As a result, instead of bringing forward creative new ideas which might be quite profitable, they attempt to control clients and limit spending to predefined levels.

Clearly, traditional bureaucratic processes are not working well. Generally, the result is an ugly combination of low-payoff work, a lack of strategic alignment, higher costs, poor quality, fractured partnerships with clients, poor teamwork, ruined careers, and an ineffective organization.

(Other than that, everything's fine!)

Traditional resource-management processes result in low-payoff work, a lack of strategic alignment, higher costs, poor quality, fractured partnerships with clients, poor teamwork, ruined careers, and an ineffective organization.

It would be easy to believe that such problems are "inevitable," as if that's just the way businesses work. Staff, no doubt, feel victimized by their situation and powerless to change it.

In fact, leaders are far from powerless. This book describes a scientific basis for designing effective resource-management processes, as well as the practical mechanics of how things should work.

4. Perspective:
An Economy Within Corporations

At the core of all the problems described in Chapters 2 and 3 is a common thread: money. 5 Problematic politics, relationships, teamwork, and culture are all just symptoms. The root cause is the way resources are managed.

The answer is not simply giving your organization more money. When products and services are seen as valuable, there's no limit to clients' wishes. No matter how big your budget is, clients' demands will always exceed available resources. With a bigger budget, all the same problems will still occur, just on a larger scale.

The answer is not simply expecting executives to make better financial decisions. Resource decisions are endless; they arise on a daily basis at every level of an organization. The truth is, for lack of time and attention, no individual executive or high-level committee can hope to do an adequate job of making every decision, no matter how smart they may be. To even attempt to do so is interfering with management, not improving it.

The right answer is systemic change. These problems can be solved effectively, once and for all, by *changing an organization's resource-management processes* so that the right decisions are made by the right people, without executive intervention, day after day.

Resource-management processes are complex. It's naive to think that these problems can be solved by a quick fix such as a steering committee or by jumping headlong into chargebacks.

This chapter provides the foundation for a comprehensive solution, one that's well grounded both in science and in pragmatic organizational realities.

---

5.   Staff's time and infrastructure capacity are also resources; but they too are
      ultimately a function of available money.

Business-Within-a-Business Paradigm

Every organization within a corporation can be viewed as a business within a business, selling its products and services to internal and external customers. 6

Typically, only a few organizations serve outside customers directly. They, in turn, depend on the products and services produced by other organizations within the company — their internal "suppliers."

Every organization within a corporation can be viewed as a business within a business.

Consider an example: A product manager is responsible for the profitability of a product line.

She hires Marketing to understand customers' preferences, and Engineering to design her products.

She buys manufacturing services to produce them. Manufacturing, in turn, needs help from Manufacturing Engineering to prepare its plant to make the product.

The product manager buys marketing programs to promote her product, and motivates the sales force to sell it.

Meanwhile, experts in Finance, IT, HR, Facilities, Administration, Law, etc., provide their products and services to everyone.

---

6. For more on the business-within-a-business paradigm, see: Meyer, N. Dean. *An Introduction to the Business-Within-a-Business Paradigm.* Ridgefield, CT: NDMA Publishing. 2002.

This is a *value chain* within a company.

In this context, every organization is in business to "sell" products and services to clients in a marketplace that comprises the rest of the corporation (and in some cases to external customers).

(The word "sell" doesn't necessarily mean that money changes hands. This language simply reminds us of a customer-supplier relationship.)

This market (the rest of the corporation) is complex. Each business unit is unique in its mission and in its role in corporate strategy, and hence has unique objectives. As a result, each internal client has unique requirements of its internal service providers.

"A market is a collection of individual decision-making units, some of which desire to buy (demand) and some of which desire to sell (supply) a particular good or service."

— Robert Haveman and Kenyon Knopf [7]

To address these diverse needs, internal service providers offer a range of products and services. Some may be operational — necessary, but not very glamorous. Others may have tremendous strategic potential.

Every group exists because its work is valuable, and every function has some strategic potential. In other words, every function is an interesting and worthwhile line of business.

7.   Haveman, Robert Henry and Kenyon A. Knopf. *The Market System*. New York, NY: John Wiley & Sons. 1970.

Competitive Marketplace

A business within a business faces fierce competition from outside vendors, contractors, and consultants — *outsourcing* vendors who make every effort to attract clients away from internal service providers.

By the way, life isn't fair. While outsourcing vendors may invade internal markets, the opposite may not be true. Internal service providers may not be encouraged to sell their products and services outside the company. External sales must be in keeping with the strategic business directions of the corporation.

Outsourcing vendors aren't the only threat. Competition also takes the form of clients who choose to support themselves (perhaps even hiring their own support staff) rather than buy from the corporate provider, i.e., *decentralization.*

A few internal functions may be granted a monopoly. Common examples include corporate telecommunications, physical facilities, and employee compensation and benefits. Everyone is required to work with these corporate providers.

But the surest way to lose a monopoly is to behave as a monopolist. Even in these cases, the best leaders recognize they must *earn* clients' business by providing good value and great customer service.

Budget Versus Revenues

It's easy to understand the concept of earning revenues by delivering products and services when organizations charge clients directly for their work. But what if you don't charge back, and instead are given your own budget at the beginning of each year?

Most people believe that your budget is yours to spend. In fact, it's not.

In the business-within-a-business paradigm, budget is provided so that clients can buy things from you. If the budget is given directly to you (put in your accounts), it represents a *pre-paid account* — money which belongs to clients but is put in escrow with you at the beginning of each fiscal year. Then, throughout the year, clients use it to buy your organization's products and services.

You incur expenses (like salaries) in the course of producing products and services for customers. When you deliver the results, you are "paid," perhaps from this pre-paid account or perhaps through chargebacks.

In other words, you must *earn* revenues to cover your expenses by delivering results to customers.

Your budget represents a *pre-paid* account — money which belongs to clients but is put in escrow with you at the beginning of each fiscal year.

Out of your revenues, you've got to cover both your direct and your indirect expenses. To do so, you must price your products and services in a way that covers support services and overhead.

Typically, a business within a business doesn't make a profit. It charges at cost rather than at market rates.

Nonetheless, when an internal service provider delivers products and services with a value to the business greater than their costs, it's creating a profit for the corporation's shareholders. This profit just appears on its clients' books rather than its own. (Had they paid market rates to an outsourcing vendor, this profit would have accrued to the vendor's shareholders instead.)

Definition of the Internal Economy

Since every organization exists to serve customers within a market, the laws of economics apply to functions inside of corporations just as they do to corporations inside of nations. For example:

When price is zero, demand approaches infinity.

The study of economics is hardly so simple. But a simple fact remains: If your products and services appear free, clients are likely to demand far more than your available resources can produce.

In spite of these overwhelming demands, the truth is, your corporation can afford to buy only a finite amount of your products and services.

You are not the constraint; the corporation's spending power is. Limits on its spending power constrain what your business within a business can do.

You are not the constraint;
the corporation's spending power is.

With its limited resources, a corporation must somehow decide what products and services each business within a business produces, and who gets them. This mirrors what a national economy does.

An organization's internal economy drives the following resource decisions:

*   How much spending power (budget) is allocated to each function.

*   Who controls that spending power (sets priorities and makes purchase decisions).

*   How much is reinvested to keep an organization up to date and to augment its capabilities.

*   How resources are tracked and how people are evaluated.

The internal economy includes all the resource-management processes that make these decisions — from budgeting, through prioritization of expenditures, to accounting and management metrics.

The internal economy includes all an organization's resource-management processes.

The goal is, of course, to produce just the right amount, type, and quality of each product and service so that the corporation's scarce resources are spent in a way that maximizes strategic alignment and returns on investments.

The Role of Chargebacks

When people hear the term "internal economy," some mistakenly assume that it means chargebacks — internal transfer payments for services rendered to other organizations within the corporation.

This misconception may scare people away. Before going any further, we need to set the record straight.

First, let's recognize that executives' concerns about chargebacks are well-founded. The truth is that most chargeback systems have caused more harm than good.

In looking at the many examples of failures of chargebacks, there's a common thread: Bad experiences occur when chargebacks are installed for the purpose of cost accounting without considering the broader design of an internal economy.

Clients accustomed to a free resource resist having to pay for internal services. Everyone naturally wants everything for free, and clients resent staff if it appears they're taking this "right" away.

Worse, since the many other aspects of a market economy aren't implemented at the same time, chargebacks in these organizations often have little impact on decision making. Business units are stuck with the organization's costs after the fact, without meaningful control over purchase decisions (priorities).

Charges that are outside their control do little good and create ill will. It's natural for these clients to see chargebacks as bureaucratic and offensive.

It's also natural for them to fight back. They question the charges and accuse the organization of being overpriced. These controversies damage the partnership between an organization and its clients.

Resentment is especially strong if chargebacks are installed but an internal monopoly is maintained — that is, if it is difficult for clients to use *their* money to buy services elsewhere. They may feel they are being victimized by high costs, with no recourse but to pay anything the provider asks.

Meanwhile, internal service providers may not be ready to earn clients' business. It's one thing for financial staff to calculate prices; it's quite another for the managers within an organization to to perform as effective internal entrepreneurs.

Staff may not have defined their products and the specific deliverables within each, and may not know how to develop convincing proposals, produce clear invoices, or compete in an open market.

A headlong rush to chargebacks can lead to even more serious problems.

A headlong rush to chargebacks can lead to serious problems.

The introduction of chargebacks clearly creates an understanding of the costs of a function. However, if clients don't understand the value of the function to them and to their business strategies, chargebacks will chase clients away. Clients may not even buy products and services that are, in fact, good investments.

Even if clients understand the value of the organization's products and services, they may not appreciate the value added by buying it through the internal service provider. Instead, they may work directly with external vendors (outsourcing) or do the work themselves (decentralization).

These alternative sources typically cost the corporation more, although that truth may not be readily apparent. Clients' decentralized staff or outside contractors may appear cheaper because clients don't consider (or track) the full cost to the corporation of their work (e.g., overhead on their own staff and the costs of managing contractors).

Furthermore, clients may not understand the hidden costs of decentralization. Consider this case example:

A Corporate IT department found that, after it introduced charge-backs, clients began hiring their own IT experts.

It appeared cheaper to do so because clients had not considered the true cost of systems, including documentation, training, project-management time, and ongoing maintenance.

They also hadn't considered the true cost of IT experts, including housing them, equiping them, and managing them.

Clients also didn't consider the value of architectural compliance and the quality controls built into the methods of the Corporate IT department.

The result was many little IT groups scattered around the company.

Naturally, there was loss of economies of scale and replication of efforts, resulting in a confusing array of disparate technologies that were costly to maintain and virtually impossible to integrate. Costs rose and synergies were lost.

Furthermore, these small decentralized groups, all trying to cover the entire range of technologies, became generalists who could not keep up with technology innovation. Corporatewide, the pace of technology innovation slowed. For lack of anyone tracking these new technologies, they never could know what opportunities were missed as a result.

Meanwhile, the corporate IT group was relegated to supporting "common" applications and shared infrastructure. There was little it could do to deliver strategic value. In fact, it wasn't even able to save the corporation money by building solutions for specific business units using common platforms and reusable code.

With career paths shattered and opportunities for exploring new technologies limited, the good staff drifted away. Over time, the entire IT function deteriorated. Eventually, the company turned to outsourcing, paying a vendor a hefty profit to do what it had failed to do — manage a healthy IT organization.

In this case study, chargebacks weren't the only problem. But they were the catalyst that triggered a caustic reaction that ate away at profits and careers.

There have been other cases where clients understand the value of both the products and of good staff support, but still choose not to do business with the internal service provider because it's not sufficiently customer focused. Staff may fail to offer clients alternatives, instead insisting that that they know what's best for clients; they may even treat clients as nuisances rather than valued customers.

For any or all of these reasons, the premature and isolated implementation of chargebacks often results in sudden, drastic, and inappropriate downsizings of corporate staff.

But the good news is, chargebacks are *not* required to make an internal economy work.

Chargebacks are not required to make an internal economy work.

The mechanics of creating a market effect without chargebacks is explained in coming chapters.

Limits to the Metaphor

We mustn't take the business-within-a-business paradigm too literally. There are some differences between an internal economy and a national economy.

A market-based internal economy does not imply capitalism — that is, private ownership of the means of production. Clearly, all assets belong to the corporation. In an internal economy, we define "moral ownership" as the right to control the disposition of an asset, even though the legal owner is the corporation.

Similarly, a market economy does not mean that employees' compensation is solely based on how well they fare in the internal marketplace. Unlike independent entrepreneurs, one's personal savings are not at risk. While performance appraisals may be linked to people's success as internal entrepreneurs, financial results are just one input to an evaluation process that must consider staff in a broader context.

Nor does a market mean that anyone in the firm can go into any line of business they wish. Management retains responsibility for the organization's structure (who's in what business), and for hiring, promoting, and firing people.

The application of a market system within corporations is strictly focused on the processes by which budgets are determined, production volumes of various products and services are set, and priority and project-approval decisions are made.

It's a means of coordinating the complex set of activities that together add up to the functioning of an organization.

What's At Stake?

Viewing resource-management processes through the lens of a market economy brings into sharp focus the problems illustrated in Chapters 2 and 3. Consider this analysis:

Pat's corporation is run by a "central soviet" — the corporation's executive team. *Budgets are given directly to each internal service provider organization to produce its products and services.*

This fundamental mistake undermines any market mechanisms.

Clients aren't limited in their spending power, and don't get to decide what products and services they receive. Instead, internal service providers like Pat's are expected to set their own priorities, fending off clients' demands to stay within their budgets.

Of course, clients — like all customers — resent being disempowered. They blame staff when they don't get all they want, and relationships become contentious.

Meanwhile, staff scramble to deliver all they can and neglect their own needs.

Eventually, the confluence of unconstrained demands and little reinvestment in themselves or in client relations destroys organizations' capabilities, their reputation, and their businesses — just like the mess left by the Soviet economies of the 20th century.

The result: higher costs, lower payoff, lost strategic opportunities, slowed innovation, strained relationships, and burned-out staff.

Clearly, the people involved — both clients and Pat's staff — are not to blame. These problems are systemic. They're rooted in the design of the organization's internal economy.

The Solution

With the application of *market economics* within organizations, resource-management processes can be sorted out decisively, once and for all.

When resource-management processes are designed based on market principles, clients understand that they have limited money to spend on internal service providers. Instead of loudly demanding more than staff can produce, they use their limited spending power wisely, buying from staff what they need the most.

Staff earn revenues to cover their costs, not from their boss in the form of budgets, but rather from their internal customers by selling their products and services. They are empowered to run their businesses within a business as customer-focused entrepreneurs.

The right people make informed decisions dynamically throughout the year, and staff's products and services are continually aligned with the changing needs of the business.

A marketplace can be implemented within corporations with or without actual chargebacks. The key is *giving control of spending power to clients, and letting them decide what they will and won't buy from internal service providers.*

We all know that markets work in the broader world of national economies. In the next chapter, we begin an exploration of how to engineer the "perestroika" of an organization.

5. Mechanics: Four Components of an Internal Economy

Like cogs in a machine, all the mechanisms within an internal economy must mesh.

For example, even if chargebacks are in place, myriad decision processes, policies, and tools are required to ensure that prices actually drive effective decision making. If any of the necessary pieces are missing or are out of sync, chargebacks may amount to nothing more than cost accounting (and an administrative nuisance).

The internal economy comprises an organization's budgeting, pricing, purchase-decision (priority setting), and resource-tracking processes.

To work properly, an internal economy must be designed as a total system so that every dollar flows to its best possible use, controlled along the way by those in the best position to make financial decisions.

To do this, leaders need a "big picture" view of all the components of a practical internal economy and how they fit together.

In this and the next four chapters, we turn our attention to the mechanics — the specific processes that add up to an internal economy.

Figure 1: Internal Economy Subsystems

Budgeting: filling up checkbooks; the annual (or semi-annual) processes that decide how much the corporation will spend on each function.

Pricing: determining unit costs (rates) by identifying the right units, assigning direct costs, and amortizing indirect (fixed) costs.

Purchase Decisions: writing checks; the project-approval processes that assign budget to projects and services, adjusting priorities dynamically throughout the year.

Tracking: accounting processes that provide information for decision making and evaluation, both for pursers and for providers.

Figure 2: Budget-by-Deliverables Spreadsheet

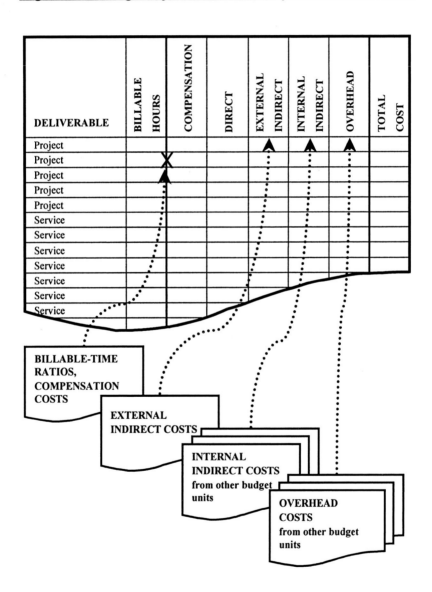

Figure 3: Market Effect Without Chargebacks

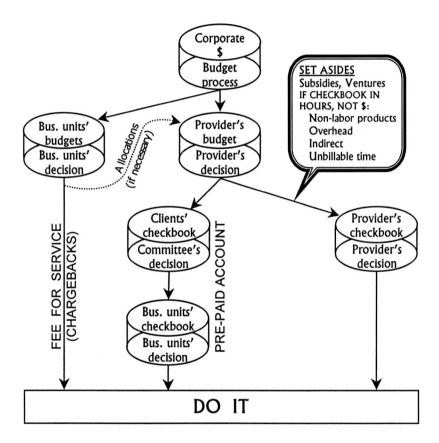

Figure 4: Summary of Benefits

Financial:
* Right level of budget
* Flexible budgets
* Strategic alignment
* Cost control
* Less inappropriate outsourcing and decentralization
* Competitive pressure
* Appropriate reinvestment

Cultural:
* Entrepreneurship
* Frugality
* Customer focus
* Contracting
* Empowerment
* Teamwork
* Quality

At the highest level, there are four interlinked subsystems that make up an internal economy. (See Figure 1.)

*   Budgeting
*   Pricing (rate setting)
*   Purchase decisions (priority setting)
*   Resource tracking (accounting)

These four subsystems give leaders a framework that defines what's involved in redesigning an internal economy.

In a chapter on each, the subsystems are defined and market-economics principles are applied to explain how they *should* work.

6. Budgeting: Filling Checkbooks

Definition

The budgeting subsystem contains the processes by which a corporation decides how much to spend on an internal service provider.

Budgeting *creates spending power* by setting aside money to be used to buy an organization's products and services. Essentially, the budgeting subsystem fills up "checkbooks."

Budgeting and Chargebacks

Where chargebacks have been implemented, an organization's budget is determined by how much its internal clients choose to spend on its products and services.

> With corporatewide chargebacks,
> a budget process is only used to
> move profits out of "cash cow" divisions
> into growth divisions that need investment,
> and into corporate-good activities
> which further enterprisewide synergies.

The organization may still develop a "budget" for client products and services, but it's not a true budget in the sense of a checkbook of money that can be spent. It's a forecast of revenues and expenses that helps managers plan their spending for the coming year.

More broadly, where chargebacks have been implemented throughout an entire corporation, money flows into the corporation through those few organizations which serve external customers (such as product managers). They buy what they need from support functions, and pay for these products and services. In this way, everything else is funded by the flow of money from external customers through the corporation's internal value chain.

In these (rare) cases, a corporate budget process is only used to move profits out of profit-generating divisions into growth divisions that need investment, and into corporate-good activities which further enterprisewide synergies. This is a "redistribution of wealth" to fund corporate strategies (just as countries redistribute wealth to achieve social objectives).

But what if every internal service provider doesn't charge clients for its products and services? In this case, the budget process is a way to move money from the primary receivers (who serve external customers directly) to fund the various support functions throughout the corporation.

Without corporatewide chargebacks, a budget process moves money from the primary receivers (who serve external customers directly) to internal support functions.

For these, the vast majority of organizations, an effective budgeting subsystem is especially important.

How Much?

A few months before the fiscal year begins, corporate executives meet to consider budget proposals and determine how to allocate the corporation's expected revenues and capital, i.e., decide how much the corporation will spend on each function.

A corporation can only afford a finite amount of money for each internal service provider. When the budgeting subsystem is working well, it designates just the right amount of spending power for each.

What is the right amount?

Theoretically, an organization should be funded up to the point where all the really good opportunities (both ongoing services and new projects) are approved, and the next-best investment offers a return that is just below the corporation's weighted-average, risk-adjusted cost of capital.

This would maximize shareholder value, but it assumes the corporation is willing to acquire more capital if investment opportunities warrant.

In practice, a corporation continues to add money into an organization's budget until the next best expenditure isn't as attractive as investment opportunities elsewhere in the corporation.

The "right amount" is when the marginal returns on investments are roughly equal in all the various organizations throughout the corporation. This optimizes returns when there's a fixed amount of money to be distributed. *8*

In simple terms, an organization offering great payoffs gets more budget, the money coming from reductions in the budgets of organizations where the opportunities aren't as lucrative.

8.   In Keynesian economics, this is termed "dynamic equilibrium."

Budget-by-Deliverables

To support this decision process, executives need to understand their investment opportunities, both the costs and the payoffs. The budget subsystem must supply this information.

To do so, organizations present budget requests in terms of the cost of proposed deliverables (totalling the rows rather than the typical budget for cost factors by group). This is termed an "activity-based budget," or a "Budget-by-Deliverables"(R). 9

An activity-based budget lists all the possible projects and services — deliverables — that clients might wish to buy from the internal service provider. Each deliverable represents a distinct purchase decision.

For each deliverable, there is an estimate of its full cost, not just its direct (marginal) cost. (See Figure 2.)

Overhead and other indirect costs — so-called "fixed" costs, the ongoing costs of doing business which are not in themselves deliverables — are imbedded in the prices of each deliverable.

Internal service providers manage their indirect costs in light of competitive pressures. The management hierarchy scrutinizes assumptions in the spirit of frugality, and coaches its staff on the right level of indirect expenses.

Note that these are decisions made within the organization. Indirect costs are not separately funded and are not subject to debate by the organization's clients during the budget process. Ultimately, internal service providers are measured by price comparisons with competitors.

Thus, clients don't tell staff how to run their businesses. They only choose which deliverables they'll buy.

9.   For more information, see: Meyer, N. Dean. *An Introduction to Activity-based Budgeting*. Ridgefield, CT: NDMA Publishing. 2002.

Deliverables may include both capital and operating expense. While these two types of money are kept separate throughout the process, they are planned together to remain synchronized. It does no good to be given capital without the expense budget to implement and support it, or vice versa.

All costs of everyone involved in delivering projects and services are aggregated, building teams across the entire organization in the process.

A budget by deliverables lists all the possible projects and services that clients might wish to buy, and the full cost of each.

Client, Subsidy, and Venture Deliverables

There are three types of deliverables that are presented in a budget:

* Client projects and services
* Subsidies
* Ventures

Client: Client deliverables are products and services that benefit specific business units (or consortia of business units).

The bulk of an internal service provider's revenues typically comes from its clients, whether through chargebacks or via the organization's core budget (the "pre-paid account").

While all deliverables are fully costed with their fair share of indirect expenses, the costs of client deliverables do *not* include funding for things the organization does for the good of the entire corporation or for itself: Subsidies and Ventures.

Subsidies: Separate line items decribe "Subsidies" for deliverables which benefit the corporation as a whole which competitors (out-sourcing vendors and decentralized staff) don't do.

For example, corporate staff may spend time facilitating consensus on policies and standards. They may survey vendors and recommend certain products and configurations for the company (like a "consumers report" service). They may coordinate their professional peers in decentralized staff groups. They may be involved in corporatewide community-action initiatives.

Since Subsidies for these corporate-good activities are explicit budget items, internal service providers are not put at a disadvantage vis-a-vis external competitors (outsourcing) and decentralization as they would be if these costs were buried in the prices of their products and services.

Furthermore, corporate executives can make rational decisions about how many such services to fund.

Subsidies may continue indefinitely, as long as the need remains.

Ventures: Separate line items are also included in the budget for "Ventures," investments in the capabilities of the organization itself.

This includes capital for infrastructure, funding for research and development of new lines of business, and transformations that will significantly improve the effectiveness of the organization or are necessary to meet regulatory requirements.

These investments are made for specific improvements for a finite period of time. For example, if the Venture funds are to launch a new service, they continue until the new service is self-supporting (providing revenue-producing client deliverables).

Funding For Infrastructure

As just mentioned, infrastructure is funded by budget for Ventures, not by including the cost of new infrastructure in project budgets.

Clients are charged for the *use* of infrastructure, not for the purchase of infrastructure. Providers include the depreciation of the infrastructure in the cost of operational services (which are client deliverables).

Of course, there are costs beyond depreciation related to the infrastructure. The internal service provider must also pay for ongoing operations, repairs, necessary changes (enhancements), and ultimately disposal. All these life-cycle costs are included, along with depreciation costs, in the price for infrastructure-based services.

By moving infrastructure capital costs out of project budgets and into distinct Venture rows, clients understand that providers own the infrastructure and have the authority to consolidate and rationalize its total capacity.

With this change, executives learn that there's a big difference between the numbers in a budgeted deliverable (one year's budget) and those in a project proposal (which include life-cycle costs).

Budget Decision Process

The mechanical change of budgeting by deliverables brings with it substantive changes in the budget negotiation process.

An internal service provider proposes a budget that describes *all* the things clients have requested, not just what its managers think will be approved.

Of course, this may add up to twice what's affordable for the corporation. But it's not up to staff to judge clients' requests and trim the budget, counter to customer focus and entrepreneurship.

Exactly what the corporation will and won't buy from internal service providers is a business decision made by corporate executives.

Executives fund deliverables based on strategic alignment and returns on investments. They understand that, when budgets must be trimmed, it's *their* job to decide which deliverables the corporation will do without (rather than pressuring staff to promise more than they can deliver under the "do more with less" rubric).

Budget negotiations shift to a businesslike discussion of what the corporation will and won't buy from the organization.

Instead of micro-managing the organization by deciding its travel and training budget, executives debate the value of the proposed deliverables and make fact-based investment decisions. While corporate executives may coach and manage performance through-out the year, during the budget process they behave as customers, not bosses.

Operational deliverables are scrutinized in the same manner as new projects.

This process inherently implements zero-based budgeting. Budget decisions are based on the possible investments in the coming year, not arbitrary benchmarks like prior year's budgets. The past is used as a benchmark only for routine, ongoing operational costs.

During the process, clients justify the projects and services that benefit them, rather than expecting their internal service providers to justify spending corporate money on the things clients want.

Note that since clients are the beneficiaries of the proposed investments, they have an incentive to do a good job of supplying all the information executives need to make good decisions.

This way, decisions are based on clients' deep understanding of their business strategies and how the proposed investment will help them achieve those objectives. This gives executives far better information for decision making.

Budgets are zero-based, with decisions based on the returns on investments in the coming year.

Providers propose and justify Subsidies for their corporate-good activities. Since these items are explicitly funded, not buried in the cost of client deliverables, executives can make informed decisions about which such corporate initiatives are truly worthwhile.

Providers also propose and justify Venture funds for infrastructure and self-improvement. They develop business plans, market forecasts, and convincing business cases for their proposed investments.

Where the Budget Goes: Checkbooks

If an organization charges clients for its work, most of its budget is channeled to its clients — business units who consume its products and services. This kind of organization must earn its revenues through chargebacks.

But even with full chargebacks (full cost recovery), some budget is always given directly to the internal service provider for Subsidies and Ventures.

On the other hand, if an internal service provider does not charge clients for its products and services, budget is given directly to the organization, the traditional approach.

Even in these cases, a market effect can still be created.

As described in Chapter 4, the internal service provider's budget can be treated as a pre-paid account — a checkbook that really belongs to the organization's clients. It will be up to clients to decide how to spend that checkbook throughout the year (as described in Chapter 8).

Mechanically, once budgets are determined, the money is put into "checkbook" accounts rather than distributed among provider managers. These checkbooks may require new cost centers.

A policy statement describes the kinds of purchases that are eligible for funding by each checkbook.

Whether the checkbook is carried on the clients' books (real chargebacks) or on the books of the organization, a market effect can be created.

In practice, the budget process may fill up more than one checkbook, each designated for a different purpose. At a minimum, separate checkbooks are created for client deliverables, Subsidies, and Ventures.

Optionally, a checkbook may be created for each business unit, empowering each to manage its own priorities rather than having to work through a corporate committee. The size of a business unit's checkbook is determined by the products and services for that business unit which were approved during the budget process.

Corporate executives may review the distribution of funds, perhaps quarterly, to adjust to changing investment opportunities across business units.

During the Year

If and when clients want more than the original budget supports, staff willingly supply it... at an additional cost. The additional funding is provided either by clients paying costs out of their own budgets (chargebacks), or by mid-year adjustments to the provider's budget (and hence to the client's checkbook).

Mid-year budget adjustments are not limited to fixed dates. Avenues are available whenever warranted to present investment opportunities and gain more funding. Thus, budgets are adjusted as needed throughout the year to meet the changing needs of and investment opportunities in the business.

A mid-year budget revision reflects all the same decision processes as the annual budget process, although it may focus only on adjustments rather than a zero-based review of all deliverables.

Bottom Line

A healthy budgeting subsystem creates checkbooks based on the investment opportunities known at the time budgets are decided. It then allows flexibility throughout the year as business conditions change.

Often, a redesign of the budget process simplifies it.

For example, funding channels for large, mid-sized, and small investments are integrated. Large and small projects alike are funded by the same checkbook, and are subject to purser approval.

This eliminates any incentives to break projects into little pieces to circumvent scrutiny. It improves returns on investments (ROI) by allowing pursers to put all investment opportunities, large and small, new and ongoing, side by side and pick the best. An integrated decision process also avoids distortions, e.g., approving low-payoff small projects because the money is there while higher-payoff larger projects go unfunded because that checkbook is empty.

As another example, most corporations track capital investments separately from period expenses. Tracking them separately is wise. But investment decision-making must consider both together since deliverables may require both capital and operating expenses. These two "colors of money" are decided in an integrated budget decision process.

Once a Budget-by-Deliverables is approved, clients understand exactly what they can expect from an internal service provider. As a result, it's not staff's fault if they can't meet every demand. Clients know exactly what's funded; and if they want more, they know they have to justify incremental funding.

There are no incentives to use up the budget if good investments aren't available; nor are there incentives to spend less than is in the budget by forgoing good investments. The return of excess money at year end does not prejudice next year's budget, nor is it rewarded, since next year's budget is forward looking and zero based.

The net effect of all these changes is better budget decision making, leading to improved returns on investments and strategic alignment.

7. Pricing:
Planning Indirect Costs

Definition

The pricing subsystem attaches costs to each product or service.

Prices (i.e., rates) are unit costs (like cost per hour), as distinct from the total cost of projects and services described in a budget.

Prices Exist With or Without Chargebacks

Prices are necessary to make market economies work, and exist in some form in every internal economy, with or without chargebacks.

Pricing is obviously relevant where clients are directly charged for their purchases.

Prices are calculated, consciously or indirectly, whether the organization charges clients directly or is funded through a core budget.

Pricing is equally relevant when there are no chargebacks and the provider is funded through its own core budget. In its budget, an organization agrees to deliver a set of products and services for a given amount of money. By comparing the deliverables to the budget, a price can be imputed.

For example, if a provider receives a budget of $20 and promises two units of work, the imputed price is $10 per unit.

Thus, prices take one of two forms:

* Chargebacks are actual unit prices, billed to clients for each purchase decision.

* Without chargebacks, prices are inherently decided in the budget process, based on how many products and services an organization promises for a given amount of budget.

In other words, prices are calculated, consciously or not, whether an organization charges clients directly or charges the pre-paid account created by its budget.

Allocations

Pricing is different from allocations. Pricing attaches a cost to individual purchase decisions made by clients.

Allocations, on the other hand, are charges to business units based on high-level formulas, typically calculated after the fact.

While allocations may be useful for cost accounting purposes, they have little impact on economic decisions. Since they don't communicate the cost to shareholders of each project or service, allocations don't help clients make fiscally sound purchase decisions within their finite spending power.

Furthermore, since any single purchase has little effect on the overall allocation, the cost consequences of their demands may be imperceptible to clients.

Pricing, by contrast, attaches a cost to each individual purchase decision. Thus, prices guide clients to make the best use of their scarce spending power.

Importance of Pricing

Some think of pricing as simply a means of assigning the costs of a service function to the various business units — as a matter of cost accounting.

It's true that pricing affects the allocation of costs to business units. If costs are not properly assigned, one business unit may pay more than its fair share while another gets a free ride.

With that said, it's not too tough to set prices based on primary cost drivers. If cost accounting were your only objective, simpler is better, as long as prices are equitable and defensible.

Pricing attaches a cost to individual purchase decisions.

In fact, pricing does much more than allocate costs to business units.

Pricing is a way to communicate to decision makers the cost to shareholders of their investment options. When combined with benefits estimates, prices gives clients the information they need to judge returns on investments, decide what's economic and what's not, and determine how to spend the corporation's limited resources in the best possible way to maximize shareholder value.

Prices are also critical to balancing supply and demand. They tell providers how much to charge to a checkbook, which determines when that checkbook is used up.

If only a subset of the costs are charged to a checkbook (whether via chargebacks or decrements to the pre-paid account), then clients will be able to buy more than the provider has resources to deliver.

In other words, under-pricing induces demand in excess of supply, which leads to disappointed clients and burned-out staff.

Prices also allow entrepreneurs to expand their businesses when clients are willing to provide additional funding to buy more of their products and services. When they expand, proper pricing gives them all the resources they need to deliver the additional work (including funding for support services and for growth in indirect costs).

Pricing is a way to communicate to decision makers the cost to shareholders of their investment options.

From this market-economics perspective, the selection of the items on the price list and the assignment of costs to each item are critical determinants of an organization's contribution to shareholder value and its long-term viability.

Marginal-cost Pricing

Some have suggested that internal service providers allocate their fixed (i.e., indirect) costs to the business units or fund them via core budget, and then charge clients for only the marginal costs of the work they do for them.

They believe this is simpler (it is), and that it will more accurately recover fixed costs (also true).

However, marginal-cost pricing leads to a number of serious problems:

*   Marginal-cost pricing sends inappropriate price signals to the internal marketplace. By implying that products and services are much cheaper than they really are, it induces customers to buy more than is economic for shareholders.

*   Marginal costs cannot be compared to competitive benchmarks. This covers lots of sins. The internal service provider can be very inefficient and still appear cheaper than external vendors who must amortize indirect costs in their prices.

*   The organization finds it difficult to expand support services and infrastructure as its business grows, since increasing the allocation is extremely controversial.

    This creates bottlenecks on client deliverables, and forces the primary delivery staff to do work that could be done by less-expensive or more-specialized support staff.

    As the business grows and support staff are stretched more thinly, the result is higher total cost, lower quality, and delays.

*   Similarly, ongoing investments in the organization's capabilities (which are, by nature, indirect), are controversial and difficult to expand as the business grows.

    Even costs as fundamental as professional development and product R&D, being indirect, are in jeopardy. They must be debated as budget items since they're not imbedded in prices, and client executives are generally quite willing to cut them.

    As a result, providers become less and less efficient over time. Ultimately, their competencies and infrastructure deteriorate to the point of failure.

*   Clients resent allocations of indirect costs that are outside their control (again, "taxation without representation").

*   Since they're billed for indirect costs (indirectly through the core budget or directly through allocations), clients believe it's their right to control decisions on them. In the process, an organization loses control over its infrastructure and internal support services.

The truth is, direct marginal costs do not represent the true long-term cost to shareholders of providing the product or service. As accountants know, nothing is fixed in the long term. The term "fixed" only refers to those costs that change in steps rather than continuously, or those that take time to adjust.

For example, an IT department may have a computer server with excess capacity. Is adding one more application free? And then does the next application after that, which requires an addition to capacity, have to pay for the entire cost of another server? Should the ROI of these investment opportunities change based on the order in which they're considered?

Obviously, the straw that breaks the camel's back should not be burdened with the entire cost of a new server. Nor can the investment in infrastructure be debated in isolation of clients' demand for services that utilize it.

To bring all the right information to bear on decision making, every application on that server should bear part of the total cost of the server.

More generally, even when costs rise in a step function (e.g., where capacity is bought in chunks), each customer should pay a fair share of the total cost of the assets used.

Full-cost Pricing

In a healthy internal economy, prices are based on full activity-based cost accounting — the true long-term cost to shareholders of each service.

Prices incorporate a fair share of indirect costs — both the so-called "fixed" costs and other indirect support services.

In entrepreneurial terms, revenue-producing sales to customers must be priced so as to cover all the many unbillable activities within the group and throughout the organization as a whole.

Prices are based on full activity-based costs, the true cost to shareholders of each service.

In setting prices, managers determine what indirect costs are imbedded in the price charged for each product or service, i.e., they decide how much overhead is to be burdened on each sale.

For example, if the organization charges $10 and the direct cost is $8, then only $2 remains to contribute to overhead. If this overhead is entirely consumed by necessities like management, salary burdens, and support services, there may be nothing left to fund the time and expenses for training, product research, and writing proposals for new projects.

In other words, the pricing subsystem determines how much money (and time) is available for crucial unbillable activities such as product research, professional development, and working with customers to develop new projects. It drives the level of investment an organization can afford to make in staff's capabilities, in client relationships, and in business effectiveness.

Indirect costs are amortized into prices in a way that ensures their full recovery at conservative levels of demand.

As an organization's business grows, indirect costs are scaled up in proportion to total revenues. In this way, support services and infrastructure capacity are allowed to expand in proportion to the overall organization.

If the business grows, indirect costs may be over-recovered — in the short term — but in the long term, this is fair since no costs are truly fixed.

Pricing drives the level of investment an organization can afford to make in staff's capabilities, in client relationships, and in business effectiveness.

Billable-time Ratios

A key type of indirect cost is staff time spent on unbillable activities such as product research, professional development, and meeting with customers to develop new business.

After setting aside time for these important sustenance activities, the percentage of an employee's total hours per year that's available to work on deliverables is called the "billable-time ratio."

In the process of calculating prices, each manager sets a target billable-time ratio that's reasonable for his or her particular line of business. Billable-time ratios are higher (and overhead is lower) in commodity-products groups where their products and services are relatively stable and customers' needs tend to be similar.

The greater the pace of innovation, the more research and development is needed and the lower the appropriate billable-time ratio is.

Similarly, the greater the degree of customization, the more time will be needed working out contracts with new customers (business development, which is generally not billable), and the lower the appropriate billable-time ratio.

Blended Labor Costs

Labor costs are based on a blend of employees and contractors. This mix is planned in advance, along with the various costs and billable-time ratios of each.

This leads to the calculation of a blended cost per hour of compensation, a key component of pricing.

This blended compensation cost is applied equally to all projects. This way, provider managers are free to staff each project with the optimum mix of employees and contractors without affecting charges to clients.

Price List

With or without chargebacks, an internal service provider publishes a price list.

Publishing a price list doesn't necessarily imply chargebacks. Charges can be made against the pre-paid account (core budget) in lieu of chargebacks.

When well chosen, the items on the price list (the units of sale, i.e., "price per *what*") are understandable, controllable, measurable, and at the right level of detail. Each item on the price list represents a meaningful purchase decision.

Rates are applied consistently to all clients, even if some clients pay chargebacks and others benefit from the organization's core budget.

The same rates apply both to budgeted deliverables and to incremental fee-for-service work. Consistency ensures equity, and eliminates distortions in decision making due to misleading prices which vary from true cost.

When the new price list is introduced, clients are educated so that they understand how it was calculated and how it compares to outsourcing vendors.

In particular, they must understand that raw contractor costs cannot be compared with staff who are housed, equipped, and managed by the internal service provider.

Rates are explainable, understandable, and equitable.

The price list is not revised too frequently, providing a stable environment for clients to plan investments and to manage their checkbooks.

Bottom Line

The overall results of an effective pricing subsystem are: an open, rational calculation that's equitable, defensible, and not subject to political pressures; and prices that are comparable to outsourcing vendors.

Indirect costs are appropriately funded, and are automatically scaled up as a business grows.

Furthermore, by clearly communicating the true costs to shareholders of purchases, prices give clients the information they need to make fiscally sound investment decisions.

8. Purchase Decisions: Writing Checks

Definition

Once budgets are established and checkbooks have been filled, the purchase-decisions subsystem "writes checks" for selected projects and services.

Remember that checkbooks (created by the budgeting subsystem) may be within clients' business units, in which case an organization charges for its products and services.

Alternatively, an organization may get a core budget and hold the checkbook within its accounts. In this case, no chargebacks are required, but someone still must write checks out of the pre-paid account.

In either case, the purchase-decisions subsystem sets priorities among competing investment opportunities and determines which requests will be funded.

Dynamic Process

The separation of the budgeting subsytem and the purchase-decisions subsystem is key.

Although the budget process may decide some of the larger investments before the fiscal year begins, business conditions change. Priorities cannot be locked in a year in advance. They must be adjusted throughout the year.

In a healthy internal economy, the year may begin with the priorities identified during the budget process, but the purchase-decisions subsystem adjusts priorities as business needs shift throughout the year.

In other words, budget decisions examine available investment opportunities *once a year* to determine the right amount to put in checkbooks; then *throughout the year*, the purchase-decisions subsystem decides how to spend those checkbooks.

While the budget process fills checkbooks once a year, purchase decisions are made throughout the year.

This separate purchase-decision process is key to an internal service provider's responsiveness. As business strategies change, resources always flows to the best available investments, and the organization continually stays aligned with clients' most pressing needs.

Note that the organization's resources may not go to the projects and services that were discussed during the budget process. No one should be held at fault if budgets are "reprogrammed" to better investments during the year.

In summary, filling up checkbooks (by looking at what one *might* spend) is not the same as writing checks. While the budget process fills checkbooks once a year, purchase decisions are made throughout the year.

Pursers

Someone must be given the signing authority for each checkbook and the responsibility to adjust priorities as needed throughout the year. We call this person (or committee) a "purser."

A purser is designated for each checkbook. Pursers decide how the finite resources in their checkbooks (money and time) are utilized (i.e., spent on the organization's products and services). They write checks.

A purser for each checkbook writes checks (sets priorities).

When properly chosen, pursers are fair representatives of their beneficiaries.

Most of an organization's budget is intended to fund products and services for clients. The internal service provider certainly should *not* be the purser for this portion of its budget.

Appointing an organization as purser for its own budget disempowers its clients — the business units — who then cannot control all their factors of production, and hence cannot really be held accountable for their results (despite all the rhetoric on autonomous business units).

It also undermines relationships by setting up the provider as a hurdle rather than a customer-focused partner.

Furthermore, the provider acting as the purser for the clients' checkbook doesn't make sense. It would be like giving a vendor your money and asking it to decide what you'll buy!

Instead, clients (business units) appoint pursers who manage this portion of the organization's resources. In fact, in most corporations, clients are clamoring for control over internal service providers' priorities, and have no hesitation to fulfill this purser role.

With clients as pursers, even when the budget is carried on the books of an internal service provider (i.e., no chargebacks), clients make purchase decisions within their finite spending power. (See Figure 3.)

Purchase decisions are made by representatives of clients, not by providers.

Client pursers are senior executives within business units who have a deep understanding of their business strategies and know how to use the internal service provider's products and services to achieve them.

Consider the common steering committee, comprising client executives, whose role may not be all that clear. A good use of it might be to serve as the purser for the clients' checkbook.

Alternatively, the client pursers may be individual executives in each of the business units. In this case, the client checkbook is divided into a small checkbook for each business unit.

Pursers have no say over what other business the internal service provider may engage in or how the organization is managed. In other words, client pursers do not review everything the organization does. They only manage their own checkbooks.

It's important to note that a purser committee is distinct from a steering committee that serves as an organization's internal "board of directors." Pursers are customers. Their role is strictly to set priorities within a given budget, not to oversee the organization. These two types of committees should never be mixed.

For other portions of its budget, the internal services provider is its own purser. Pursers are named within the organization to manage Subsidies, Venture funds, and overhead. They make decisions for these resources without the need for client approvals (though of course subject to the oversight of their management hierarchy).

Purser Accountabilities

Serving as a purser requires knowledge and skills. In a well-implemented internal economy, the powers and accountabilities of pursers are clearly specified in a policy statement. Beyond that, pursers are offered training in the internal economy's processes and in any necessary analytic skills.

Pursers make themselves available frequently to review clients' proposals and to adjust priorities in a timely manner. They may meet monthly with the clients they represent, as well as make mid-month decisions whenever needed.

(Where there are chargebacks, priorities are set daily whenever any empowered client decides to spend his or her own budget on the organization's products and services.)

Pursers spend their checkbooks wisely. They review money remaining in their accounts and decide how best to spend it.

This is where the concept of "portfolio management" is applicable.

With portfolio management, pursers consciously decide the mix of products and services they'll buy from internal service providers with their limited checkbooks, just as they do when managing a portfolio of financial investments.

Pursers carefully consider competing requests for funding, examining returns on investments and strategic alignment. This means they need to know the full cost of each proposed deliverable, as well as the expected payoff of each.

Through their involvement in purchase decisions, pursers learn to be "smart buyers" and compare internal service providers with their external competitors on an "apples to apples" basis. They learn the value of quality-related attributes, such as policy compliance and security, which may be routine for internal service providers but cost more outside.

Pursers, not providers, are held accountable for the return on investments in an organization's products and services.

Corporate executives typically don't have time to review every purchase decision. But they do review the performance of each purser periodically (e.g., quarterly) to decide if the money they gave to that purser to manage was used wisely and the returns warrant filling up that purser's checkbooks for the coming period.

Provider Proposals

To help pursers make informed purchase decisions, staff produce informative and well written proposals.

Proposals clearly and precisely define the planned deliverables.

Proposals describe viable and meaningful alternatives, and include all the information about each alternative that pursers need before they make a decision. By offering alternatives, providers don't preempt pursers' right to choose how to spend their checkbooks.

Proposals include comprehensive and realistic time and cost estimates (including all internal subcontractors), both for the initial acquisition and throughout the life-cycle of the investment. This way pursers learn to manage their discretionary resources with consideration of future life-cycle costs (which they'll later have to pay), even though future year's operational costs are not represented in the current year's budget.

Client Advocacy

Clients justify their requests to their pursers, presenting business cases based on their deep knowledge of how the product or service will help their business units succeed.

Internal service providers may help clients present their requests to pursers by costing proposals.

Staff may also help clients define the benefits, including the strategic impacts and quantification of both cost-displacement and value-added benefits. [10] But the internal service provider doesn't try to explain clients' strategies or defend clients' needs.

Ultimately realizing the potential benefits requires more than just buying a product or service. Clients must make good use of that product or service, often requiring changes in their business practices. Clients, not the provider, are accountable for these business changes.

Thus, in addition to expected benefits, pursers may also require clients to demonstrate their commitment to the needed business changes before approving the investments in internal service providers' products and services.

Note that client pursers only set priorities among the products and services they buy. Since internal service providers sell only billable hours (not full-time people), unbillable time is prioritized by provider managers, not clients.

The organization also sets its own priorities within available funds for overhead, Subsidies, and Ventures.

---

10.   Cost and resource information is generated automatically by an internal economy. Value estimates require additional methods. For information on measuring strategic benefits, see: Meyer, N. Dean and Mary E. Boone. *The Information Edge*. Ridgefield, CT: NDMA Publishing. 1987.

Consortia

Internal service providers are never their own customers, even in cases of enterprisewide projects. Instead, clients band together to form "consortia."

From the internal service provider's perspective, a consortium acts as a single customer. Members agree on what they'll buy, how they'll pay for it, and how they'll use it.

If separate client checkbooks are assigned to each distinct business unit (one form of internal economy), pursers pool their spending power to share the costs and ownership of investments that benefit them all.

The clearer that clients' understanding of their consortium agreement are, the less likely problems are throughout the project. Instead of sending conflicting signals to the internal service provider, members of the consortium work out their common requirements and speak with one voice.

Over and above what they get through the consortium, individual members of a consortium may buy additional things to satisfy their unique needs. These constitute distinct projects, deliverables separate from those bought by the consortium, and must be separately funded by the individual business units.

Internal service providers may offer to facilitate the formation and operation of client consortia, but they are not members — they are not their own customers.

Contracts

Pursers' purchase decisions are documented in clear contracts between the internal service provider and its clients.

These internal contracts are not legal documents, but rather clear mutual understandings of the accountabilities of both a customer and a supplier.

Contracts are not big omnibus agreements established once a year to cover any and all purchases (sometimes mislabelled "service-level agreements"). Instead, a clear mutual understanding is documented for each distinct purchase decision.

Internal contracts document both providers' and customers' accountabilities for each distinct purchase decision.

A service-level agreement (SLA) is a contract for a specific service covering a period of time.

Service-level agreements for ongoing services can be approved annually, but nonetheless are within the purview of the clients' pursers. This permits pursers to trade off operational services with new projects. For example, they may wish to stop the operation of old services which are of marginal value to free resources for new projects.

SLA's are only appropriate when the quantity and quality of a service can be decided a year in advance.

For example, an SLA is appropriate for any ongoing service, but it's not appropriate for repairs (which can vary widely in scope throughout the year). Emergency repairs are handled by a standing agreement with the purser that pre-authorizes immediate work, but not by an SLA that offers an unknown quantity of service for a fixed price.

Supply/Demand Balance

All purchase decisions for all products and services are funneled through the appropriate pursers.

No client work is done without a purser funding it. This ensures that pursers' decisions are respected.

All clients and staff understand this policy. Clients learn to work through their purser rather than just pressuring staff to do their projects.

When pursers run out of money (or hours), no more work can be approved or done.

Through education, it's clear to staff and clients which activities require purser approval (all client-benefitting projects and services), and which are done at the discretion of the provider (unbillable activities).

Of course, pursers must limit their spending to available resources. Contracts are not approved unless a purser can afford to pay for the work.

When pursers run out of money (or hours), no more work can be approved or done. They can only approve deliverables within available resources.

Thus, supply and demand are automatically in balance; expectations exactly match available resources. This is the key to eliminating backlogs, to controlling costs, and to ensuring that expectations match available resources.

Bottom Line

The purchase-decisions subsystem is a key driver of shareholder value. By ensuring that the highest-payoff opportunities rise to the top of the stack, it has a powerful impact on returns on investments and on strategic alignment.

The key to success is a client-driven decision process. The right pursers, fair representatives of the beneficiaries, control each checkbook. And decisions are made dynamically throughout the year (not just once a year).

The overall result of an effective purchase-decision subsystem is a simplified, unified decision process that improves strategic alignment, provider flexibility, client satisfaction, teamwork, and returns on investments.

9. Tracking:
Accounting and Metrics

Definition

The fourth (and final) subsystem of an internal economy is tracking.

The tracking subsystem includes conventional accounting systems. The most significant changes in accounting systems are driven by the shift in control of budgets from providers to pursers.

Budgeted funds flow into checkbook accounts, not provider managers' cost centers. As pursers buy the organization's products and services, money is transferred out of these checkbooks and into revenue accounts in managers' cost centers.

The tracking subsystem also includes all the various financial reports that track the status of an internal economy,

The foremost purpose of these reports is to give those making decisions the facts they need to do their jobs well. An important second purpose is to help others evaluate the performance of these decision makers.

For both purposes, appropriate metrics are essential.

The key to effective measurement is this: Metrics must match what people can control.

Thus, this chapter separately discusses tracking systems for pursers and for internal service providers, each of whom controls a different set of decisions.

Pursers' View

Pursers are responsible for deciding what to do with available resources. To do so, they must be aware at all times of the balance in their checkbooks.

Checkbooks: The view of a budgeted amount that dwindles to zero by year end — the traditional type of accounting report — is appropriate for pursers who manage checkbooks (not for internal service provider managers).

Pursers see budgets (checkbooks) that dwindle to zero by year end.

Encumbrances: A significant portion of a checkbook may be obligated by past purchase decisions (operational services to "keep the lights on" and projects already underway). Thus, pursers also need estimates of *encumbrances,* invoices they can expect in the future due to their past purchase decisions. Only the remainder (the total in the checkbook minus encumbrances) is truly discretionary.

One might ask, why even give pursers the money for encumbrances, when it's only going to be subtracted from their available spending power right away?

Doing so allows clients to understand why an internal service provider's total costs are as much as they are.

Keeping an eye on encumbrances also encourages clients to eliminate operational services that are no longer needed, releasing resources for more-important new projects. *11*

---

11.   It's up to an entrepreneurial provider to figure out how to redeploy its resources in response to such shifts in market demand.

It also helps pursers understand the importance of life-cycle costs, not just acquisition costs.

To make pursers aware of encumbrances, providers shift their attention away from forecasting expenses for the remainder of the year for each cost factor, and instead forecast expenses for the remainder of the year for each contract.

Invoices: To know where their spending power is going, pursers get clear invoices that show charges for work completed. Invoices are generated based on the organization's published price list and on metrics of deliverables (staff's time and other services).

A data-collection mechanism captures all billable activities as they are delivered. This includes automated data from equipment-based services, and job tickets (or time cards) filled out by staff. Staff at all levels are educated on exactly what activities are billable (and wind up on an invoice) versus unbillable.

All direct costs, such as project-specific vendor purchases, are tracked to contracts.

Invoices are at the appropriate organizational level (by purser, not by each individual client within a purser's business unit).

Invoices are readable, and clearly linked to purchase decisions. They are not overwhelming in detail. If additional detail is required, the internal service provider can break invoice line items into their component charges, allowing the purser to understand the source of all charges.

For projects that extend across multiple months, invoices cite project milestones. Pursers need to be aware of progress to maintain their confidence in the internal service provider's invoices and delivery capability.

When pursers form consortia to share costs (as described in Chapter 8), invoices are divided among multiple pursers in the proportions decided by the members of the consortium.

If pursers don't understand or agree with invoices, there's a process for explaining and adjusting charges.

In addition to current invoices, reports that summarize past spending help pursers plan future budgets.

Pursers' Metrics

Pursers are evaluated based on how well they utilize their budgets.

First and foremost, they must not spend more than they have in their checkbooks.

In addition, pursers are accountable for the returns on their investments, which they determine when they set priorities and decide which proposals to fund.

Measuring pursers by their ROI requires metrics of payoff as well as cost. Metrics of payoff are more difficult to produce. Periodic studies of actual investment returns may have to substitute for ongoing reports to pursers.

Whether or not pursers are measured financially, they are certainly measured by the satisfaction of the clients they represent.

Providers' View

Managers within an internal service provider need a very different view of the data.

Each group within an organization is treated as a business. Like any entrepreneurship, it begins the year with *no* budget. It spends money to produce products and services, and receives revenues for those deliverables to cover its costs.

Thus, managers do not receive traditional budget reports of planned versus actual expenses and budget remaining. Instead, they see "profit-and-loss" (P&L) statements that juxtapose their expenses with the revenues they receive from pursers for their deliverables. The net total is equivalent to a corporation's bottom line.

Providers see profit-and-loss statements that juxtapose expenses with revenues.

On the revenue side of their P&L, managers see payments that represent the price of the deliverables they've sold to customers. Where chargebacks have been implemented, revenues are easy to track. But even without chargebacks, staff still collect revenues from the pre-paid account (the organization's core budget).

On the expense side, managers see their compensation expenses, direct costs of projects, indirect costs paid to outside vendors, and indirect costs paid to other groups within the organization or elsewhere in the company. This expense tracking is generally not too different from traditional accounting systems.

Providers are charged depreciation on their assets (such as infra-structure). As a result, when a manager decides to buy an asset, he or she considers total life-cycle costs of ownership.

In some companies, asset owners are expected pay interest on the capital tied up in un-depreciated assets. Doing so balances the demand for capital with the corporation's available supply.

Depreciation and interest are, of course, built into the rates for the services produced using that infrastructure. This way, customers ultimately pay for their fair share of the infrastructure they use, and providers' revenues cover their costs.

To associate depreciation and interest charges with the right group, an organization maintains a "balance sheet" which tracks assets (capital infrastructure) by owner within the organization.

Providers can also produce profit-and-loss statements by product line to improve their product-management abilities.

Providers' Metrics

Internal service providers are not measured by the value of their work to the corporation, because payoff is primarily controlled by clients. Client pursers decide what to buy, and an internal service provider cannot force pursers to buy the right things.

Furthermore, clients themselves decide how to make use of their products and services. An internal service provider certainly cannot force clients to make good use of its deliverables.

Thus, internal service providers cannot control the payoff of their work. Evaluating an organization based on the business value of its products and services would be grossly unfair. [12]

Instead, providers' metrics focus strictly on how well they run their businesses.

Provider managers are *not* asked to justify differences between forecasted and actual expenses by cost factor, the traditional metric.

If an entrepreneur wins more business than planned, the organization is free to expand its supply (e.g., through contractors) to match

---

12.   Often, the executive in charge of an internal service provider is held personally accountable for the strategic alignment of the function. This is inappropriate for two reasons: As described above, alignment is determined primarily by clients' purchase decisions, out of the control of the provider in a healthy internal economy. Second, to the extent that the internal service provider can help clients discover high-payoff opportunities, this is the job of internal "account representatives." The top executive cannot be the only sales representative for the business within a business.

funded demand. When this occurs, expenses *should* exceed forecasts (but so should revenues), without the stigma of a "negative variance."

Conversely, provider managers are not rewarded for positive variances (spending less than planned by turning away business).

Instead, provider managers are expected to break even, that is, to match actual expenses to the actual revenues they receive for the products and services they deliver.

(In certain cases, managers are expected to do better than break even and generate a profit, particularly where internal service providers sell to clients outside the corporation.)

If revenues exceed expenses (a profit), a manager may be producing more than his or her resources permit. Either staff are burned out with excessive workloads, or they are producing shoddy work (or both). Reports showing an unexpected "profit" can help justify additional headcount.

On the other hand, if clients spend less during the year than expected, revenues shrink. The provider must figure out how to reduce expenses accordingly (regardless of what was in the original budget).

To keep their expenses within these reduced revenues, managers shift staff among groups. "Temporary duty" is one mechanism, where people are loaned from one group to another within the organization to help with temporary peak loads. Retraining may be needed to address permanent shifts in the market.

If managers don't reduce expenses to match lower-than-expected revenues, their P&L will show a negative net (a loss) that they'll have to explain.

Thus, the profit-and-loss statement is a metric as well as a management tool.

Flexible Supply, No Caps

Note that an organization's annual budget is not a guaranteed level of business. It can change upward or downward during the year. Therefore, internal service providers continually forecast their markets, and flexibly expand (or shrink) their supply to match clients' demand.

To permit this flexibility, caps on provider's headcount and gross expense are eliminated. Caps constrain providers from growing to satisfy all funded client requests, but they don't really control corporate spending; they only chase market share to alternative (more expensive) sources such as decentralization and outsourcing.

Even without caps, there's no concern for uncontrolled costs. Clients' spending power is limited by the corporate budgeting process, and the provider's size is determined by what clients are willing and able to spend on it. No additional controls are necessary. (Spending controls are discussed further in Chapter 11.)

This flexibility allows internal services providers to be entrepreneurial, suggesting new and potentially high-payoff ideas that may warrant budget increases.

Providers' Competitiveness

In addition to breaking even, internal service providers can (and must) produce their products and services more efficiently than their competition.

Their price list — directly comparable to external vendors — is one key indicator of their efficiency.

A provider's actual billable-time ratio is another key indicator of business performance. It should be neither too high nor too low (as discussed in Chapter 7). Actual billable-time ratios can be reported monthly, and should approach a pre-determined target.

Providers can also be measured by their market share, a telling indicator of customer satisfaction. These are not monthly accounting reports, but rather are periodic studies of an internal service provider's revenues as a percent of total corporate spending on its function (the total including decentralized staff and outsourcing).

Other Tracking Tools

Beyond financial accounting systems, other tracking tools help managers operate effectively in a market-based internal economy.

Resource planning tools (such as calendars or project management systems) are utilized to plan and track projects, reserve time for emergency work, and set aside some hours each week for unbillable activities.

A database of contracts documents all client and internal-customer agreements for all products and services. This helps providers track their commitments and identify when their staff will become available before they make any new promises.

Bottom Line

In summary, the tracking subsystem supports two very different views:

* It gives pursers the ability to manage their checkbooks, and gives executives tools to evaluate pursers.

* It gives internal service providers the ability to manage their businesses, and their executives tools for evaluating their performance.

The total effect of changes in the tracking subsystem is comprehensive cost control and effective utilization of resources, producing information that's relevant to what people can control.

10. The Payoff: Shareholder Value

Implementing an effective internal economy is a lot of work. What makes it worth your while?

First and foremost, it improves bottom-line results. It controls costs better. It enhances corporatewide strategic alignment. And it improves the quality of financial decision making.

Furthermore, a market-based internal economy solves real problems by replacing cumbersome, time-consuming, frustrating processes with practical, sensible, and useful processes. It eliminates bureaucracy.

A market-based internal economy solves real problems and improves bottom-line results.

It also provides more effective means of governance. It doesn't pit staff against their clients to control spending. And it precludes the need for disempowering micro-management.

There are monetary benefits from better strategic alignment. There are relational benefits when staff fulfill every promise to clients without having to control them. There are motivational benefits from rationalizing demands on staff and from empowering managers to run their businesses within a business.

Beyond all this, a market-based internal economy improves the culture of an organization, encouraging customer focus, entrepreneurship, and teamwork.

All these benefits can be sorted into two categories: financial, and cultural. This chapter reviews both the financial and cultural benefits to staff, their clients, and the enterprise as a whole. (A summary is provided in Figure 4.)

Financial Benefits

The obvious benefits are financial: A marketplace makes smarter decisions about the use of money and time; and in doing so, it improves the corporation's bottom line.

A marketplace makes smarter decisions about the use of money and time.

Specifically, it drives the following critical financial decisions:

*   **Right level of budget:** Activity-based budgeting gives executives the information they need to make financially sound investment decisions during the budget process.

    Budgets are based on the actual investment opportunities at hand. Executives' depth of understanding of the benefits of proposed investments is greatly enhanced since clients defend their needs for the internal service provider's products and services.

    Also, an activity-based budget provides explicit feedback on the cost of corporate-good programs, permitting objective decisions about their value.

    The right level of budget means that money won't be wasted on poor investments just because an organization was given that much money last year. Conversely, if there are good invest-ment opportunities, they won't be missed just because they add up to more than last year's budget.

Activity-based budgeting is zero-based budgeting at its best.

* **Flexible budgets:** Business units may estimate their require-ments in the annual budget cycle. However, new business needs which arise during the year won't be rejected just because they weren't planned.

If clients perceive the need for investments beyond pre-set budgets, they're able to move resources from other areas into the needed function (e.g., from marketing to IT, or vice versa), or to increase their spending (as long as they can justify the investment).

This optimizes the corporation's returns by dynamically channeling scarce resources to the best possible uses.

* **Strategic alignment:** Establishing client pursers empowers business units to control the priorities of support staff.

Clients buy what they most need, and not those products and services which aren't as relevant to their success. As a result, strategic alignment is virtually automatic.

Even better, this alignment process occurs continually through-out the year, without having to wait for periodic strategic plans or executive intervention.

* **Cost control:** Pursers have to limit their purchases to their available spending power. Providers have to match expenses to the revenues they receive from pursers. Thus, the corpora-tion has complete control over spending without constraining the size of the internal service provider's organization.

Beyond this, there are incentives for saving money.

When less is spent on a project than anticipated, pursers have the right to use the remaining money for other things. This encourages them to choose less expensive alternatives (once the project has progressed to the point of understanding technical options), trading off marginal features on budgeted projects for more-valuable new capabilities elsewhere.

Or, if they choose not to spend the savings, there's no penalty for not using up their budget since next year's budget is zero-based.

The overall effect is cost control, incentives for frugality, and yet flexibility when great investment opportunities warrant increased spending.

* **Less inappropriate outsourcing and decentralization:** As money moves to the best investments available at any point in time, provider organizations expand (or shrink) their delivery capabilities to meet demand without any artificial constraints on headcount, capital, or gross expense.

This eliminates an artificial reason for expensive alternatives such as outsourcing and decentralization. Entrepreneurs use external resources when they're more economical, but clients aren't forced to use vendors or hire their own staff, even when they're more expensive, just to get around self-imposed constraints on an internal service provider's size.

Also, by keeping this incremental business in-house, internal service providers maintain their market share, enhancing staff's career opportunities and gaining economies of scale.

* **Competitive pressure:** A marketplace provides incentives for, and metrics of, staff's efficiency.

Outsourcing vendors may bid a subset of an organization's deliverables at a cost lower than the organization's total budget. But, of course, to compare apples to apples, the organization must isolate that same subset of its deliverables.

With an activity-based budget, fair comparisons are possible because the total budget is broken out by deliverable.

Also, it's easy to compare internal service providers with out-sourcing vendors since staff assign prices (based on full costs) to their products and services.

This competitive pressure enhances efficiency and saves money.

* **Appropriate reinvestment:** The market automatically seeks the right balance between short-term savings and investments in the organization's long-term viability.

Providers control their costs to remain competitive. But they do spend an appropriate amount on support services (overhead) and invest in their future capabilities through processes of innovation.

Since clients are forced to work within their finite checkbooks and their expectations are held within internal service providers' available resources, staff are not routinely over-worked and underappreciated, and don't sacrifice their own needs to satisfy unconstrained customer demands.

They have time to keep their skills, products, and infra-structure up to date. They have time to work with customers and respond to their inquiries, and to explore new business opportunities. And they have time to fulfill normal manage-ment processes that sustain the business without jeopardizing project delivery.

Thus, internal service providers remain efficient and effective in the long-run. And, of course, staff do a better job when they're not burned out.

All this leads to lower turnover, more innovation, and more satisfied and productive staff.

In summary, financial benefits include improved returns on investments, strategic alignment, innovation, productivity, reduced turnover, and cost savings.

Cultural Benefits

In addition to financial benefits, a well-designed internal economy can make significant contributions to an organization's culture:

* **Entrepreneurship:** One of the most fundamental differences in a market-based internal economy is that internal service providers are treated as businesses within a business. This brings out staff's entrepreneurial spirit.

    Staff aren't responsible for controlling clients' spending. If clients really want something, they can give the internal service provider more money to do the work (assuming they can justify the incremental budget).

    Staff use this incremental money to expand their businesses, perhaps hiring contractors or utilizing vendors. Growth indicates customers' satisfaction and willingness to buy from the provider — a sign that its products and services are worthwhile and a good value to the business.

    In this environment, staff are encouraged to be creative and suggest new, high-payoff ways in which they can improve their businesses and better serve their customers.

    This is the essence of an entrepreneurial spirit.

    The payoff is seen in engaged staff who put a lot of creative thought into maximizing their contribution to the corporation.

*   **Frugality:** Along with being creative, entrepreneurs are
     naturally frugal. They keep their costs down to remain
     competitive.

     Beyond this, there are no incentives for maximizing one's
     expenses (empire building).

     In the traditional financial environment, both approval for an
     investment and the funding to cover it come from the boss.
     Managers introduce new products and services by getting
     approval to spend more money (e.g., hire the additional staff).

     Of course, approval for an additional expense does not, in
     itself, bring in more revenues.

     In a market-based internal economy, new business opportuni-
     ties are handled differently. Instead of trying to convince their
     boss to increase their operating budget, entrepreneurs take on
     more expenses only when their revenues are sufficient to cover
     them.

     When they wish to introduce a new product or service, they
     first establish the market by making some sales, fulfilling them
     with vendors or contractors. This puts the minimum money at
     risk.

     Once they become convinced that the paying demand is stable
     or growing, contractors are replaced with permanent staff.

     There are situations where entrepreneurs need capital invest-
     ments (Venture funds), which is a budget that comes from
     one's boss. But here too, their business case is based on
     forecasts of market demand.

     When staff manage their businesses by profit/loss statements
     rather than budgets that they consider their own, they naturally
     become frugal, and base their spending on expected revenues.

*   **Customer focus:** The transfer of control of the budget from internal service providers to pursers who represent clients has a huge impact on culture.

When budget comes from one's boss, it's natural for staff to think they own the budget and to believe they can decide what to do with it. They magnanimously accept clients' input to *their* decisions. But they believe they should do what *they* think is best for the corporation. This way of thinking is the opposite of customer focus.

But when money comes from one's clients (whether through chargebacks or through treating core budget as a pre-paid account controlled by a client purser), staff clearly understand that they must please clients to earn their business.

As a result, staff respect clients' purchase decisions, and they treat clients well to keep them coming back for more.

Customer focus is also enhanced because staff escape the "bad guy" role of judging clients' ideas and telling customers "no" for lack of budget. Staff are not an approval hurdle, and are never asked to restrict clients' access to the organization's products and services in order to limit them to pre-determined levels of spending.

Meanwhile, clients understand that their pursers must work within their finite checkbooks. If their purser doesn't approve a project, clients know that this is their business unit's decision and they don't blame staff for the inevitable limit on their available resources. This, too, enhances the image of staff as customer-focused entrepreneurs.

Thus, a market-based internal economy induces a high degree of customer focus, demanding that providers serve (not control) their clients, respond to clients' priorities, and earn clients' business through performance and attitudes.

*   **Contracting:** When clients decide to buy a product or service from an internal service provider, they and the provider establish an explicit contract.

Contracts document their understanding of mutual accountabilities, and lead to more effective project teams with fewer misunderstandings and disputes. They avoid wasting efforts working on the wrong things, or on continually expanding projects that never end ("scope creep").

In addition to less confusion and lower project risk, expected benefits are more likely to be realized since both clients and staff know what they need to do to make each project a success.

Contracts also allow a provider to know its commitments, so that managers can determine available resources before they take on more work.

Contracting is a cultural practice that makes sense regardless of the design of an internal economy. Contracting is implemented as part of the roll-out of an internal economy, and is reinforced by the market paradigm.

*   **Empowerment:** The essence of empowerment is matching authorities and accountabilities, and managing people by results without telling them how to do their jobs.

A market-based internal economy does just that.

In a market-based internal economy, staff have the authority to plan and manage their businesses as they see fit. (They are, after all, the most qualified people in the corporation to do so. That's why they're in those jobs.)

They can reinvest in their capabilities and infrastructure, and can sponsor business proposals that will enhance their value to the firm. Through the appropriate level of reinvestment, an appropriate rate of innovation is maintained. Staff remain the vendor of choice and continue to deliver exceptional performance in the future.

Clients are also empowered. They have control over their factors of production, including internally provided products and services.

Of course, with authority comes accountability. A healthy internal economy clarifies accountabilities, both customers' and providers', for every aspect of resource management.

It holds staff accountable for delivering their products and services at a fair price and for the success of their businesses. Staff are managed by results — customer satisfaction and revenues that match expenses — rather than tasks.

It holds clients accountable for utilizing providers' products and services wisely.

Without any lapse in cost controls, a market-based internal economy naturally induces empowerment of both staff and clients.

* **Teamwork:** A market-based internal economy enhances teamwork, since all groups within an internal service provider face the same priorities — those set by pursers.

When pursers fund a project, they fund the entire team (not just prime contractors). As a result, differing priorities, or a lack of the needed resources in support groups, are never an obstacle to teamwork. When the prime contractor approaches a peer within the organization for help, he or she is treated as a paying customer and gains the same respect and level of service as do external clients.

In addition, a share of indirect costs and overhead are funded by each sale of a deliverable. Through this linkage, as the business grows, support services grow proportionately. This, too, enhances teamwork within the organization.

Teamwork is encouraged in another way as well:

In a bureaucracy, there are incentives to build self-sufficient "stove-pipe" groups rather than to team with peers. One's rank often depends on the size of one's budget. The more each group does for itself, the bigger it grows and the higher the manager's job-grade becomes. In these cases, there are incentives for empire building rather than teamwork.

In a market-based internal economy, the incentives are reversed. A large staff (fixed expense) is bad, not good. Entrepreneurs are evaluated by their P&L's, not by the size of their expense budgets.

As a result, provider managers minimize their fixed costs, and the internal economy gives them the tools to do so.

Staff view their peers as internal suppliers with whom they can "subcontract." Entrepreneurs prefer to "buy" rather than "make" whenever it is more economic to do so because subcontracting to a specialist gets their customer a better deal. This keeps the prime contractor's business competitive.

Note that subcontracting doesn't reduce the prime contractor's revenues — a better way to judge the size of a business (and to grade the manager's job) than by its headcount or gross expense. When jobs are evaluated by revenues rather than headcount, there's no reason to reduce a manager's job grade because he or she is better about teaming with peers or vendors.

Better teamwork eliminates redundancies and permits a greater degree of specialization, which improves efficiency, quality, time to market, and innovation.

* **Quality:** A healthy internal economy builds incentives for quality into everyone's job.

Customers choose the level of service or product features (price-point); then staff are given the resources to produce the chosen level of service or functionality to their standards of professional quality.

Internal service providers strive for excellence and do all they can to satisfy customers with high-quality results because they must earn customers' business through performance. Competition (both decentralization and outsourcing) generates pressure to ensure that they do so.

Thus, the market provides natural incentives for quality at any chosen level of service or price-point.

A market-based internal economy
induces a culture of entrepreneurship,
frugality, customer focus, empowerment,
teamwork, and quality.

Summary of Benefits

To the corporation, the most obvious benefit is improved financial decision making. This has a direct impact on the bottom line and on the corporation's ability to achieve its strategic objectives.

Clients benefit from internal service providers that are well aligned with their needs, and that clients can count on to deliver what they promise.

In addition, there are many benefits to internal service providers.

Perhaps the most noticable is that clients' expectations no longer exceed available resources. Demand and supply are in balance.

This is not to say that staff won't ever work overtime. When they're behind schedule, or when customers have an unusual and urgent need, extra effort is warranted. However, volunteering their nights and weekends without appreciation is not a fair expectation of staff nor a sustainable way of life.

Benefits accrue to the corporation, to clients, and to the organization itself.

Relief from the oppressive expectations of an impossible backlog is just the start.

In a market-based internal economy, staff find themselves in a much more exciting and supportive environment. Relationships with both clients and peers improve. Learning opportunities abound. Staff can take control of their work lives as empowered entrepreneurs, add real value to clients' businesses, and grow their businesses (and their careers) through their initiatives.

Admittedly, the benefits are tough to measure because they're so pervasive and because the changes are incremental.

Nonetheless, the payoff is significant. Investments in a healthy internal economy build effective organizations that generate long-term shareholder value.

11. Implications for Governance

While most everyone believes in a market-based *national* economy, the vision of market economics within corporations often raises a number of objections.

This chapter addresses the two most common concerns, two critical governance issues, both rooted in a fear that executives may lose essential controls.

What About Corporate Goals?

All internal service providers must ultimately support those who serve external customers. If those in direct contact with external customers aren't well supported by internal service providers, they'll be crippled in their ability to achieve the real purpose of the corporation.

This is captured in the concept of "strategic alignment" — where all organizations contribute directly to the strategic imperatives of the corporation.

Some fear that a market-based internal economy will destroy strategic alignment and encourage sub-optimizing behavior — that is, everybody pursuing their parochial objectives while sacrificing overall corporate goals. Or they believe that a cut-throat competitive spirit will destroy collaboration, and that the overall welfare of the firm will be ignored.

Experience has proven the opposite to be true.

Top-down, bureaucratic controls are more likely to encourage self-serving behaviors. Since power and money flow down from above, people naturally try to please their chain of command rather than their internal customers. Teamwork is limited to that which is mandated from above, not an automatic process, not "the way we do business."

In this environment, alignment depends on high-level strategic plans and executive interventions — processes which lack sufficient detail and which are periodic rather than dynamic.

A market-based internal economy, on the other hand, brings about far better alignment of internal activities throughout a corporation.

Described by the renowned economist, Adam Smith, as the "invisible hand of enlightened self-interests," a market automatically aligns internal service providers with the needs of their clients and of the corporation as a whole.

"Every individual endeavors to employ his capital so that its produce may be of greatest value. He generally neither intends to promote the public interest, nor knows how much he is promoting it. He intends only his own security, only his own gain. And he is in this led by an <u>invisible hand</u> *to promote an end which was no part of his intention. By pursuing his own interest he frequently promotes that of society more effectually than when he really intends to promote it."* [13]

Just as in the national economy, market forces automatically guide internal entrepreneurs to do what's best for the corporation as a whole as they look out for their own bottom lines.

The process is simple: Those who serve external customers buy just what they need from support organizations. These support organizations buy just what they need from other support organizations, and so on.

The result is alignment between clients and providers at every step in a corporation's value chain, from front-line organizations that serve external customers back through every support organization.

---

13.   Smith, Adam. *The Wealth of Nations.* New York, NY: Random House. 1937 (originally published 1776).

Even in a market-based internal economy, the risk remains that business units may be poorly aligned with corporate strategies, and that individual business-unit managers may make poor decisions. This is a matter of line management, a problem that should never be treated by staff intervention. Staff cannot force their clients to change their business directions, and they are a poor remedy for an ineffective corporate planning process or weak leadership within business units.

There is one thing client's won't buy: services which satisfy corporate goals but which don't benefit any one client. A market-based internal economy gives corporate executives the opportunity to make explicit decisions about activities that contribute to the overall corporate good.

For example, clients may not be willing to pay staff to facilitate consensus on common policies and standards. Yet, for the corporate good, policies and standards facilitate economies of scale and corporate synergies. An internal service provider's involvement in policy facilitation is funded directly by corporate executives through Subsidies rather than charged to clients.

A market-based internal economy automatically aligns support staff with corporate strategies.

Explicit funding of Subsidies gives executives clear feedback on the costs of such corporate decisions, ensuring both that the programs are worthwhile and that they get the proper level of attention.

When you look at how remarkably well a market economy coordinates companies throughout a national economy, it's easy to understand that a marketplace is the most efficient and effective means of coordinating the complex and diverse activities of people throughout a corporation. The "invisible hand" combined with explicit funding of corporate-good services align internal service providers with corporate strategies continually, in every detailed aspect of their work.

Cost Control

A second concern executives often express is a loss of control over spending.

Again, a market-based internal economy works better than traditional management controls.

In bureaucratic environments, executives expect internal service providers to control the corporation's spending on their functions. Namely, executives attempt to limit corporate spending on a function by limiting that functional area's budget.

In reality, this traditional approach to cost control doesn't work very well. If an internal service provider doesn't have the resources to satisfy them, clients who need help simply go else-where or do it themselves. And if staff attempt to intervene... well, when it comes to a dispute between a staff and a line executive, the business unit that makes money generally wins!

When staff do succeed at blocking their clients' purchases, they disempower the people who run the business. Executives cannot expect business units to be accountable for their results, and then take away their control of key factors of production. Doing so is unfair and unproductive.

Furthermore, any controlling behaviors on the part of staff puts a wedge in their relationship with clients. They are viewed as an obstacle rather than an ally. Without a close working partnership, staff find it difficult to contribute meaningfully to clients' business strategies.

Trying to control costs by constraining support staff is ineffective and short-sighted. But it is comfortably familiar.

In a market-based internal economy, this means of cost control disappears altogether.

In fact, just the opposite is true. Internal service providers are encouraged to serve clients whenever they're willing to pay.

All caps on headcount and gross expenses (real or perceived) are eliminated to allow managers to save money by optimizing the mix of employees and contractors, and to expand supply to meet funded client demands.

Is this a loss of cost control?

Absolutely not. Spending controls are not eliminated, but moved to a more appropriate and more effective place.

Instead of controlling spending by limiting the size of internal service provider organizations (supply) who in turn are expected to control their internal customers (the bureaucratic approach), the corporation limits clients' spending power (demand).

Instead of controlling spending by limiting the size of internal service provider organizations, the enterprise limits clients' spending power.

Limits on clients' checkbooks constrain providers' revenues. There is absolutely no need to cap the size of a provider organization. Its expenses are constrained by its finite revenues.

This fundamental shift in an organization's paradigm of governance allows providers to work as entrepreneurial businesses within a business. Staff are free to propose a variety of creative alternatives to their clients. Not all will be right for clients, but some may deliver huge value to the business.

Then, clients make their own decisions, occasionally even choosing a more expensive alternative than staff would recommend because a custom approach is worth the cost to that particular business.

Decisions are better informed when they're made by clients who are close to the business, aware of all the financial implications of alternatives, and accountable for their results.

Once clients make their choices, providers respect clients' decisions.

A market-based internal economy controls spending effectively without eliminating flexibility or undermining entrepreneurship.

As trust grows, clients learn to work through, rather than around, staff. In the long run, this "leading without controlling" enhances partnerships, builds staff's credibility and influence, and gives internal service providers *greater* influence over their clients' decisions, not less. 14

Ultimately, an effective market-based internal economy will control costs far better than traditional bureaucratic processes that expect staff to control their customers.

14.   This discussion applies to relationships between peer groups, not to boss-subordinate relationships. In peer relations, one group does not command or control another group. However, the marketplace in no way implies that managers cannot command their subordinates.

Not only is spending effectively constrained and decision making improved. Effective cost controls are implemented without any unnecessary dampers on flexibility or on entrepreneurship.

The Bottom Line

A market-based internal economy in no way reduces the corporate controls that align internal service provider organizations with strategies and constrain spending. Just the opposite is true. Controls are more comprehensive, adaptive, and effective.

A market-based internal economy establishes the right incentives and provides the right metrics for clients to become responsible buyers of internal services. Without loss of corporate control, business units gain control over all their factors of production without costly decentralization or outsourcing.

It also establishes the right environment for an internal service provider's staff to become self-managing entrepreneurs. By relieving them of the job of controlling their clients' spending, staff can become empowered, customer-focused entrepreneurs.

"Governance" doesn't always mean human oversight. In a healthy internal economy, many governance processes are built into the forces of a marketplace.

12. Conclusion: A Matter of Leadership

The arguments favoring market economics make good sense. And the tangible payoff is huge.

A market-based internal economy solves the problem of backlogs; ensures that priorities match corporate strategies; controls spending without forgoing wise investments; induces customer focus among support staff; empowers clients to run their business units and support staff to manage their businesses within a business; and encourages creativity and entrepreneurial initiatives.

Its impacts are far reaching, affecting critical outcomes such as return on assets and the actual and perceived value of internal support functions. It reduces costs, wasted efforts, and staff turnover. It solves problems efficiently that otherwise might have resulted in expensive decentralization and outsourcing.

The payoff will be evidenced by client satisfaction, strategic alignment, staff well-being, and the legacy of a fundamentally healthy organization.

Even better, a well designed internal economy pays off for many years to come. In this way, it's quite different from the sadly familiar corporatewide cost-cutting studies.

These top-down "slash and burn" exercises may temporarily reduce costs; but in many cases, they do not reduce some costs enough while reducing others too much. The executives and consultants who decide such cuts cannot be close enough to the business to understand all the detailed opportunities for cost savings, nor all those little investments that really are worthwhile.

Furthermore, these one-time studies do nothing to prevent unnecessary costs from rising again in the future. They don't bring about systemic changes, but rather are isolated emergency responses to years of suffering an internal economy that remains fundamentally out of control.

In contrast, fixing the internal economy will have a far-reaching and lasting effect. Through *systemic* change in an organization's internal economy, executives can impact a multitude of decisions, as if they were present to gently guide everyone at all times, forevermore.

A market-based internal economy engages every entrepreneur in managing all costs to the appropriate levels (given the needs of his or her customers) on an ongoing basis. Everyone in the firm becomes as conscious of profits as they would be if it were their own small business, so that painful one-time cutbacks are never again needed.

Beyond cost control, a healthy internal economy engages clients — those who best know the needs of their business units — in establishing the budgets of internal service providers, deciding what they'll buy with that budget, and realizing the benefits of support staff's work.

Implementing a healthy internal economy is a high-leverage use of leaders' precious time and attention.

A market-based internal economy builds into the corporate "ecosystem" a set of processes that continually optimize investments, saving money where appropriate and investing where the payoff warrants the cost.

These systemic controls don't depend on periodic plans and human oversight. They are are ubiquitious and continuous.

An internal economy does not *replace* the management chain of command. Rather, it shifts executives' focus from running day-to-day operations to coaching entrepreneurs and to facilitating and guiding the organization toward its key goals and those of the corporation.

Far from being a smaller role, executive leadership becomes more visionary and strategic — a real CEO of a business within a business.

Meanwhile, like Adam Smith's invisible hand, systemic forces gently guide everyone every minute of every day to make their respective decisions in a manner that best serves the corporation as a whole and optimizes shareholder value.

It takes deliberate thought, careful design, and meticulous planning to implement an effective internal economy.

But the benefits are compelling and far outweigh the costs. And with the flexibility inherent in its various forms, an internal economy can be designed to fit any corporate function and culture.

Systemic change in an organization's fundamental resource governance processes is a high-leverage use of executives' precious time and attention. Beyond that, it's the right thing to do for an organization, its staff, its clients, and its shareholders.

AFTERWORD: From Ideas to Action

We began this book by describing the significant and often debilitating problems that Pat, an executive in charge of a corporate services function, experienced.

We discovered that despite utilizing what many consider "best practices," these chronic problems were directly traceable to flaws in her organization's resource-management processes.

We wondered why Pat didn't take the initiative to fix these problems. Did she fail to appreciate the importance of her resource-management processes? Or didn't she know quite what to do?

The book offered a vision of the solution — a market-based internal economy. We hope it's now clear what Pat must do to succeed.

But, as is the case with all significant management innovations, just envisioning the end point is not enough to get you there.

Three pragmatic questions remain:

1. **Can the leader of an organization change his or her internal economy in isolation, or must such a change be corporate-wide and come from the very top?**

   A leader can certainly change the internal economy of his or her organization without changing the entire corporation.

   Doing so impacts others in the corporation, for example by asking clients to serve as pursers and to respect new project-approval processes. But implementation in one internal service provider organization does not depend on others implementing market economics for their organizations at the same time.

2. **Can an organization move from its current state all the way to a market-based internal economy in one great leap? Isn't this too radical a change to absorb?**

    Implementing chargebacks and a free-market economy might very well be too radical. However, there are a series of stages of evolution of an internal economy, from "Centrally Planned" (with a corporate steering committee as purser) to "Fee For Service" (a free market with chargebacks).

    Some of the in-between stages offer many of the benefits of a market without chargebacks and without significant impacts on formal accounting systems. Selecting the right stage is a key part of an internal economy implementation planning process.

3. **Is there a practical method for changing the internal economy? Just how does one get started replacing a bureaucratic morass with market economics?**

    It's hard to answer this question without speaking from personal experience. We've spent 15 years studying internal economics and implementing market-based internal economies in a variety of organizations.

    The methods that have evolved over years of practice are summarized in a companion monograph, *The Internal Economy: Overview of Implementation Processes*. It describes the stages of evolution, and the step-by-step implementation processes and tools we use both for Budget-by-Deliverables (budgeting and pricing) and for the broader internal economy systems and processes. It's available for $4.95 from:

    NDMA Publishing
    641 Danbury Road, Suite D
    Ridgefield, CT 06877 USA

    203-431-0029

    ndma@ndma.com

Index

Dean Meyer is a pioneer in applying science to the art of building high-performance organizations.

He doesn't come at it with motivational pep talks, executive training, or "touchy-feely" interpersonal dynamics. Instead, he takes a very systematic approach to designing the organizational environment that staff live in... the system of influences that make or break people's performance.

Meyer combines this breakthrough thinking with down to earth practicality, and distills leading-edge concepts into pragmatic implementation processes.

He's developed a method to change corporate culture in less than one year based on learning theory.

He's researched and applied an entirely new science of organizational structure based on cybernetics.

He's invented a tool-kit for activity-based budgeting that makes it practical for an organization to price its entire product line.

And he's been a leader in applying market economics within companies to design their resource-management processes — the "perestroika" of the modern corporation.

The result: Meyer helps leaders convert bureaucracies into vibrant entrepreneurial organizations based on the "business-within-a-business" paradigm.

Meyer is a native of San Francisco. He received a BS from the University of California at Berkeley, and earned an MBA from Stanford. He founded his consulting practice, NDMA, in 1982.